adoption
piece by piece

LIFELONG ISSUES

Edited by Sara Graefe

Published by
Groundwork Press
445 - 5525 West Boulevard
Vancouver, BC   V6M 3W6

Cover and book design by Elyssa Schmid, Radiant Design
Additional design by Jennifer Lee and Lissa Cowan

Printed in Canada by Hignell Book Printing

National Library of Canada Cataloguing in Publication Data

Main entry under title:
Lifelong issues/edited by Sara Graefe

(Adoption piece by piece)
Includes bibliographic references and index.

ISBN 0-914539-22-1

1. Adoption. 2. Adoptive parents. I. Graefe, Sara. II. Series
HV875.L53 2003   362.73'4   C2003-911056-7

*This series is dedicated to special needs
adoptive families everywhere*

table of contents

ADOPTION AND IDENTITY ISSUES

OPEN ADOPTION

SEARCH AND REUNION

ADOPTION AND SIBLINGS

foreword

This book, and the trilogy it is part of, began creative life as a concept for a booklet about adoption of children who have special needs. It was soon apparent however that there were far more issues, ideas and excellent, relevant material to be contained in a small booklet and the project scope grew to a book and when that grew too massive, finally to the current trilogy.

Each of the three books in this series stands on its own as a complete work on a particular area of adoption interest but it is all three books together that cover the spectrum of special needs adoption issues.

A project of this scope requires the effort of a great number of people to come to fruition. There is space here to mention only some of those involved. To everyone else who contributed to this project I can only express my regret at not acknowledging you directly, though you know who you are and that your contribution is greatly appreciated.

First, I must offer my thanks to all the individual article authors who have given so generously of their thoughts and work. Special thanks must go to Sara Graefe, the chief author/editor on this project. It was under her skilled and steady hand that this series actually took shape. Those thanks must also extend to our editorial and design team of Lissa Cowan, Jennifer Lee and, from Radiant Design, Elyssa Schmidt who diligently kept the work moving and gave form and life to the final product.

I want to thank the Ministry for Children and Families for their support for this project. And I especially want to thank Susan Lees of the Queen Alexandra Centre for Children's Health, Adoption Support program for her support, and the Queen Alexandra Foundation for their generous grant to support the publication of these books.

In the end though, this series was inspired by the dedication, commitment, wisdom, exhaustion and love of the families who have embarked on the life-long special needs adoption journey. The road they are on is not an easy one, but their journey is filled with hope and possibility.

It is to the families that this series is dedicated.

Brad Watson
Executive Director
May, 2003

introduction

Who We Are

In 1987, a group of ten overwhelmed parents in British Columbia came together to share experiences after adopting children with special needs. Burnt out (and often feeling burned) by systems and other organizations that didn't understand, these folks needed the reassurance and support from others *living it* that they weren't crazy or bad parents – that the challenges they were facing with their children simply came with the terrain of special needs adoption. The sense of comfort, support and community generated by these meetings was profound – so much so that these parents began advocating for similar services for other special needs adoptive families in BC. Through their efforts, the Society of Special Needs Adoptive Parents (SNAP) came into being. SNAP became a non-profit society and charity in 1988, and received its first grant from the provincial government in 1989. It was a small sum of money, but just enough to open an office and hire a few staff to get the message out that something was available addressing the very special struggles of special needs adoptive families. Call it the law of the jungle, but once that message got out, word spread like wild fire – demand for SNAP's services literally exploded and has never slowed down.

What started around a kitchen table has grown into a province-wide information, education and support service for parents, professionals, and others touched by special needs and adoption issues. SNAP has established an extensive peer support network throughout BC, with trained Resource Parents and over a dozen peer support groups, providing one-to-one and mutual support to fellow special needs adoptive parents. Through the support network, an extensive library, web site, and bi-monthly newsmagazine, along with the efforts of volunteers and an ever-growing staff, SNAP continues to ensure that the organization is accessible to all special needs adoptive families throughout the province. The Society has also established a reputation as a leading adoption resource in Canada. Over the years, we have received information requests from as far afield as Hawaii, the United Kingdom, Africa, Australia, and New Zealand.

About the Series *Adoption Piece by Piece*

Parenting any child can be challenging, even at the best of times. Parenting an adopted child with special needs presents a unique set of psychological, emotional and financial challenges. This three-volume series book speaks to the many issues faced by the special needs adoptive families and professionals in the field who access our services. Volume one explores core, lifelong issues in adoption, as well as cross-cultural and diversity issues. Volume two focuses on prevalent special needs issues that affect today's adopted children. Volume three is a toolkit for adoptive parents, providing a range of support and advocacy tips, as well as specific sections on how to advocate and work within various societal systems.

The series covers a wide terrain and strives, like SNAP's services, to provide information, education and support. The factual articles – which aim to arm you with the information you need – are interspersed with more personal perspectives from adoptive parents who are living with the issue in question, with the hope that these individual voices will help support and inspire those of you struggling with similar issues. Where possible we've tried to include pieces with a local or Canadian context. Many of the articles have been pulled from the archives of the ever-popular SNAP newsletter-turned-newsmagazine. We're also grateful to have received permission to reprint a number of articles from top American adoption specialists and publications. The result is a veritable grab bag of information, covering the whole gamut of adoption and special needs parenting issues.

What is Special Needs Adoption?
For those of you who might be new to special needs adoption, let's start by clarifying a few terms. When the public-at-large hears the word "adoption," most people think they know what it entails. In fact, they often don't – at least not in its full implications and complexities. "Adoption" typically conjures images of family, pretty much like any other family, except that the kid might not look much like Mom or Dad. We may think of loving parents who open their hearts and their homes to little ones without a permanent family – or about kids who bring the joys and laughter of childhood into the lives of couples who struggle with infertility.

Yes, adoption can certainly be these things. And of course, parents hope for the very best when they choose to build a family through adoption. But adoption is also about a whole spectrum of issues, some of which aren't always comfortable – including grief and loss, attachment issues, and identity issues to name a few. Adoption today is very different than it was 50, 60 years ago. Gone are the days from the 1950s when there were more healthy infants in need of homes than prospective adoptive families. Nowadays, the adoption of children with special needs – kids who were once considered "hard to place" or "unadoptable" – has become the norm rather than the exception. These include children with physical or mental disabilities, children with a history of abuse and neglect, sibling groups placed together, older children, and children adopted internationally.

Adopted children with special needs are extremely complex individuals who often are living with conditions and have survived traumas that are far beyond your own realm of experience. Parenting these children can be a complicated, demanding, stressful undertaking that pushes you to limits you didn't even know you had. Sometimes love isn't enough to help these children deal with past wounds or debilitating medical conditions. Special parenting strategies, interventions, and professional services and supports are often necessary.

That said, special needs adoption can also be a unique, rewarding experience. Many families have found it fulfilling for a whole host of reasons – from gaining a renewed sense of hope in the world by giving a child a home and standing by that child on their life journey, to growing stronger as a family by working together to meet new challenges. Even some of the parents who've weathered the worst pitfalls with their special needs adoptive children are still able to speak of the positives and the life-affirming experiences they've gained.

What Do We Mean by Post-Adoption Support, Anyway?

At SNAP, we recognize that adoption is a life-long process – it's not something that's over once you sign the completion papers, or the judge grants the adoption order. When you decide to bring a child into your home through adoption, you're making a lifetime commitment to that child. In many cases, you are giving a child with special needs the chance to grow up in a permanent family – to have someone there at their side as they walk through life, to hold their hand when they need support, and to have a place to call home.

Our work with families over the years has proven to us (and this has been supported by adoption research) that access to appropriate, adoption-sensitive supports throughout the lifecycle is not only desirable but *crucial*, both to meet the child's special needs and to build healthy adoptive families. And this book has been designed to reflect this philosophy. "Post-adoption support" isn't just about what to do when you first get your child home; it's about having supports in place for the rest of your lives. We've presented a wealth of information on a variety of topics that you may encounter at one point or another during your life journey with your adopted child.

Face it: our children are special. As we mentioned earlier, many of these kids were once considered "hard to place" or "unadoptable", and would have spent their childhoods in institutions. Even today, many of Canada's "waiting children" spend considerable time in high-end foster homes prior to adoption, with experienced caregivers and access to funded, specialized services to deal with their extraordinary special needs. Giving a child a permanent home doesn't take away their care requirements. Parenting these kids can be especially challenging, and you deserve all the support you can get to meet your child's needs, and to help give that child their best shot at life.

How to Use This Series of Books

There is no such thing as a "how-to" parenting manual – just as there's no single, "right" way to parent an adopted child with special needs. Each child is unique, and as a parent you are likely your own best expert on your child. These three books are here to guide you and to provide signposts along the way, as you face uncertainty or new situations, navigate troubled waters, or simply need affirmation that you're on the right path.

Each book in the series has been designed as a resource, yet another pillar in your multi-faceted support structure. (And if you're thinking, "support structure, what support structure?!", don't worry – we give you tips and ideas throughout on how to build one, or how to maintain and strengthen the one you already have in place.)

Don't let the size of the collection overwhelm you. Our intent was to cover a whole range of issues that may be encountered by special needs adoptive families. We don't expect you to sit down and read each volume from cover to cover in chronological order ("and there will be a test tomorrow") – although you can certainly do that if you like. Think instead of a grab bag, and dip in as needed, depending on what issues you are currently facing with your child. You might find it most useful to start with the chapters or sections that apply most to your own situation. That said, there may also be helpful information and strategies in other chapters that can be adapted to fit your circumstances. Remember, too, that your experiences and concerns may shift and change over time, as your child grows and changes. You may find yourself returning to certain chapters over and over again, sometimes reading the same old material with a new perspective.

The material covered in these books is just the beginning. At the end of each volume, we've included detailed resource lists, pointing you towards other books, videos, web sites, and organizations dealing with the issues covered in that section. We hope that you make use of these lists to continue to educate yourself, advocate for your child, and build a solid support structure for your family.

Keeping Afloat in Times of Change

As this book goes to press, the social services system in British Columbia is undergoing intense change. Balancing the budget while reducing taxes is the government's bottom line, and we've already seen the beginnings of massive restructuring, huge service cuts, and new user fees for services in our sector. It is hard predict what things will look like in the next six months, let alone the next six years. Naturally, this is causing a lot of anxiety for special needs adoptive parents, many of whom rely on government services, or the support of provincially funded agencies such as SNAP.

At SNAP, meanwhile, we're rapidly approaching fifteen years of service to special needs adoptive parents in BC and beyond. And we hope to be here for another 15 years – 30 years, 45 years, or as long as families continue to adopt special needs children. But the reality is, our future is uncertain. Now more than ever, adoptive parents need the tools to advocate for services and supports for their children and families, and to find creative ways to continue to build supports for themselves at a grassroots level. This book, in a sense, is our legacy to you, regardless of what happens to SNAP as we currently know it. It is our sincere hope that you will use this book as a continued source of support well into the future.

A Final Word

We'd like to thank the British Columbia Ministry for Children and Families Development, and the Adoption Support Program at the Queen Alexandra Centre for Children's Health in Victoria, for providing generous funding to assist with the creation and publication of this volume.

And we'd like to dedicate the book to the people we serve – special needs adoptive parents, and all those touched by adoption and special needs issues. We hope that this resource will help you better understand, support and appreciate your very special child.

Sara Graefe, Editor
Society of Special Needs Adoptive Parents
Vancouver, 2003

lifelong issues

Adoptive families are families like any other. At the same time, building a family through adoption *is* different, and brings with it its own set of specific issues and concerns. This is the first book in a three-part series for adoptive parents. In this volume, we focus on lifelong issues facing adoptive families, as well as cross-cultural and diversity issues in adoption.

Some Background

For many years, adoption was cloaked in secrecy and shame. Birth mothers were told to forget the children they had "given up" for adoption, while adoptive parents were encouraged to treat their adoptive children "as if they were born to" them. Legislation and social work practices at the time supported this—adoption records were sealed, and all ties with the birth family were severed.

We've grown wiser over time. Research and practice have taught us that adoption isn't a one-time event that can be easily smoothed over or forgotten. Instead, it is a unique, significant experience that touches all members of the adoption circle and reverberates throughout people's lives. Birth parents never forget about the children they place for adoption, many adopted people have a desire to learn about their roots, and families brought together through adoption *are* different.

Certainly, your adopted child *is* your very own child, but treating them "as if" they were "born" to you isn't always in your child's best interests. You undoubtedly love your child and think of him or her as family as much as you would a birth child. At the same time, adopted children grapple with a set of core issues that are specifically related to their experience of being adopted.

Grief and loss

Adopted children experience loss piled upon loss. There is the loss of that primal bond with the mother who brought them into the world, as well as the loss of their genealogy, their history, and their sense of who they are, to name but a few examples.

Adoptive and birth parents, meanwhile, have to deal with grief and loss issues of their own. For the birth family, there is the loss of a child—a child who has shared an intimate nine months with the birth mother. There is the loss of hopes and dreams for that child, and for what could have been for the birth family. For the adoptive family, there is also, in many cases, the loss of hopes and dreams, for both the parents, particularly if they are dealing with infertility issues, and for their adopted children, whose functioning may be severely impacted by special needs conditions.

And this is just scratching the surface. The toll goes on and on, around and around the adoption circle.

Attachment

Adopted children typically have difficulties attaching to their new caregivers and learning to trust. Part of this has to do with the loss of the birth mother—the person with whom they experienced that first, crucial physical bond during gestation and birth—and the grief that comes along with that. Healthy attachment for many of our kids has been further undermined during those crucial early years due to trauma, abuse and neglect, multiple foster placements before adoption, and so on. Attachment difficulties are at the root of many emotional and behavioural problems, and can be incredibly disruptive to family life.

Identity Issues

Who am I? Where do I come from? Why don't I look like my Mom and Dad like the other kids at school? As adopted children grow, they will start to ask questions. They need to process their experience of adoption at every developmental phase, and it's important for parents to consider how they can best support their child and honestly address these questions.

Other Adoption-Related Issues

Further, adoptive families are faced with a whole myriad of issues and questions that don't usually enter into the experience of those untouched by adoption. These include:

Open Adoption

Gone are the days of secrecy and shame. Here in British Columbia, legislation and practice promotes some degree of openness between birth and adoptive families. Openness can take many forms, from sharing letters or pictures through a third party after the adoption is finalized, to the birth parents visiting the adoptive family throughout the child's life. Does your adopted child have some form of ongoing contact with his or her birth family, or would you like to initiate such contact? How is this negotiated between the birth and adoptive families?

Search and Reunion

Many teen and adult adoptees are compelled to find their birth parents, often to alleviate pressing identity and/or medical concerns—how can you as an adoptive parent best support your son or daughter through this process without losing sight of your own needs and issues?

Adoption and Siblings

Adoption has impact on all members of the adoptive family, not just the adoptee and adoptive parents. What do adoptive parents need to think about when bringing an adopted child into a family constellation where there are already birth children or children from a previous adoption? What special issues do you face if you adopt a sibling group?

Disruption

We'd like to be able to say that all adoptive families are "families forever" and live happily ever after. But there are cases where, for whatever reason, the placement doesn't work out and the adoptive family has to consider relinquishing the child. This is of course incredibly painful for the child and for the family, but it may be unavoidable in spite of dedicated efforts of parents and professionals. What do you do if you think your adoption is breaking down, and disruption appears to be inevitable? Deciding to dissolve an adoption to survive as a family is one of the hardest decisions you'll have to make in your life—how do you get adequate support to help you through this difficult time?

Acknowledging that adoption *is* different is an important place to start when parenting an adopted child. By recognizing and dealing with these core issues head-on, you are working towards the healthiest outcome for both your child and your family.

Diversity Issues

While members of the adoption community share the common experience of being touched by adoption, the actual make-up of the community itself is as diverse as the rest of society. "Adoptive family" doesn't always mean white, middle-class Mom, Dad and their white adopted kids. Certainly this is one possibility—but there are also many alternatives, as families brought together by adoption are as diverse, complicated and rich as family constellations built in any other way.

Adoptive parents can include single parents, same sex couples, and older adults who are sometimes grandparents adopting their birth grandchildren. There are transracial adoptive families, some built through international adoption, others through domestic, cross-cultural adoption. There are white families raising aboriginal children, as well as aboriginal families who adopt within their First Nations communities. There are stepparents who adopt their partner's children from previous relationships. There are relatives caring for kith and kin. There are children in open adoptions who have close ties with both their birth and adoptive parents. There are children in adoptive families whose lifestyles and values conflict with those of their adoptive parents. The list can go on and on. Each variation merits acceptance and celebration as an adoptive family in its own right.

The final section in this volume aims to shatter stereotypes and redefine our perceptions of family. It includes subsections on cross-cultural issues, and the very specific experiences of single parent adoption, gay and lesbian adoption, and grandparent/older parent adoption.

Further Reading

If you've found this volume helpful, please consider reading the other two books in this series: *Special Needs* and *A Toolkit for Parents.*

For tips on how to use this book, please see the Introduction to the Series *Adoption Piece by Piece* on page 11.

Adoption Checklist:
The Top 10 Things to Do When Adopting
by Tanya Helton-Roberts & Dr. Geoffrey Ainsworth

1. Develop a self-care plan.
Parents, especially moms, often ignore their own needs and focus on those of their children. While our children are very important, we must remember that we can only give to others when we are healthy. Take the time you need to exercise, meet with a friend, have a bath, read a book, or go to the grocery store without children.

2. Find out as much history as possible.
Before your new child arrives (or the adoption papers are signed), find out as much as possible about them. Ask foster parents and social workers about behaviours you can expect and pre-plan what your response and consequences will be. Recognize that you probably will not receive all the information you need. Ask for the notes of all foster parents the child has been with. These notes should give you a better idea of what to expect. Remember that you will rarely, if ever, know everything about your child that is important. Read between the lines while preparing for the worst and hoping for the best.

3. Protect others in your home.
Many adoptive children have severe behaviour problems that parents are not expecting. They may target pets and other children in your home. Until you know your new child very well, do not leave the child alone with at-risk people or animals. Some adoptive children honeymoon for up to one year so be vigilant in watching for danger signs or suspicious activities. Trust is earned.

4. Set up a regular schedule.
Adopted children have often had multiple placements. Very little has been predictable in their lives. It will be easier for them (and you) if there is an identified

rhythm to your schedule. Develop specific routines. Post each child's list in your home with both activities and a picture demonstrating the activities.

5. Obtain respite.
Expect to need help. Investigate what services are available in your community, both public and private. Don't assume that your extended family will be able to handle the behaviours and needs of your new child. Interview and select qualified respite providers as soon as possible so that you can schedule respite times beginning shortly after the adoption.

Special Tip: Local foster parents are excellent sources of information about reputable respite providers. Consider asking foster parents about availability of their grown children to do respite work. Often these children are well qualified because of the experience they gained while watching their parents foster a wide-variety of children.

6. Request a full-assessment of your new child.
The majority of adoptive children have special needs, even if they are adopted at an early age. Ask your family physician to refer you to a psychiatrist for an assessment. If you are uncomfortable with that person, ask for another referral until you find someone you feel you can trust. Be willing to travel outside your area, if necessary. This professional should thoroughly review your child's background as well as assist you with parenting strategies specific to your child's needs. Expect to have a long-term relationship with this professional as your child moves through each life stage.

7. Have a plan to take care of the siblings already in your home.
The focus of parents following an adoption is generally on the new child. Remember that the other children in your home will continue to need individual attention. They may also be negatively impacted by the adoption. Ensure that at least a parent or an extended family member schedule specific times alone with the other child(ren). Take the other children to a counsellor or other professional to help them deal with their new sibling.

8. Prepare for attachment difficulties.
Over the past decade professionals have learned a great deal about the importance of attachment (also called bonding) and children. Separations from birth parents or primary caregivers, even at a very early age, can have long-term effects on the ability of these children to attach (bond) with adoptive parents. Learn as much

as you can about attachment and prepare for attachment difficulties with your child.

9. Expect roadblocks and overcome them.
Although parents have more resources available to them than ever before, this wealth of information can also prevent you from finding the help you need. Patient loads overwhelm doctors, government services are being cut back, and parents must work very hard to find appropriate help. Learn the words that doctors understand to describe your child's symptoms. Keep asking for help until you get it.

10. Do not tie your value as a person to the behaviour of your child(ren).
We all want the best for our children but we cannot make their choices for them. Many children who are adopted will have special needs throughout their lives and they may not ever be the 'normal' children their adoptive parents dreamt of. Your child may still need help eighteen years (or more) from now. Build a parenting plan that does not depend upon your child being a 'good' kid—you can be a successful person no matter how your child lives his or her life.

Lifelong Issues in Adoption
by Deborah N. Silverstein & Sharon Kaplan

Adoption is a lifelong, intergenerational process, which unites the triad of birth families, adoptees, and adoptive families forever. Adoption, especially of adolescents, can lead to both great joy and tremendous pain. Recognizing the core issues in adoption is one intervention that can assist triad members and professionals working in adoption to better understand each other and the residual effects of the adoption experience.

Adoption triggers seven lifelong or core issues for all triad members, regardless of the circumstances of the adoption or the characteristics of the participants:
1. Loss
2. Rejection
3. Guilt and Shame
4. Grief
5. Identity

6. Intimacy
7. Mastery/control

(Silverstein and Kaplan 1982).

Clearly, the specific experiences of triad members vary, but there is a commonality of affective experiences which persists throughout the individual's or family's life cycle development. The recognition of these similarities permits dialogue among triad members and allows those professionals with whom they interface to intervene in proactive as well as curative ways.

The presence of these issues does not indicate, however, that either the individual or the institution of adoption is pathological or pseudopathological. Rather, these are expected issues that evolve logically out of the nature of adoption. Before the recent advent of open and cooperative practices, adoption had been practiced as a win/lose or adversarial process. In such an approach, birth families lose their child in order for the adoptive family to gain a child. The adoptee was transposed from one family to another with time-limited and, at times, shortsighted consideration of the child's long-term needs. Indeed, the emphasis has been on the needs of the adults—on the needs of the birth family not to parent and on the needs of the adoptive family to parent. The ramifications of this attitude can be seen in the number of difficulties experienced by adoptees and their families over their lifetimes.

Many of the issues inherent in the adoption experience converge when the adoptee reaches adolescence. At this time three factors intersect: an acute awareness of the significance of being adopted; a drive toward emancipation; and a biopsychosocial striving toward the development of an integrated identity.

It is not our intent here to question adoption, but rather to challenge some adoption assumptions, specifically, the persistent notion that adoption is not different from other forms of parenting and the accompanying disregard for the pain and struggles inherent in adoption.

However, identifying and integrating these core issues into pre-adoption education, post-placement supervision, and all post-legalized services, including treatment, universalizes and validates triad members' experiences, decreasing their isolation and feelings of helplessness.

Loss

Adoption is created through loss; without loss there would be no adoption. Loss, then, is at the hub of the wheel. All birth parents, adoptive parents, and adoptees share in having experienced at least one major, life-altering loss before becoming involved in adoption. In adoption, in order to gain anything, one must first lose—

a family, a child, a dream. It is these losses and the way they are accepted and, hopefully, resolved which set the tone for the lifelong process of adoption.

Adoption is a fundamental, life-altering event. It transposes people from one location in the human mosaic into totally new configuration. Adoptive parents, whether through infertility, failed pregnancy, stillbirth, or the death of a child, have suffered one of life's greatest blows prior to adopting. They have lost their dream child. No matter how well resolved the loss of bearing a child appears to be, it continues to affect the adoptive family at a variety of points throughout the family's love cycle (Berman and Bufferd 1986). This fact is particularly evident during the adoptee's adolescence when the issues of burgeoning sexuality and impending emancipation may rekindle the loss issue.

Birthparents lose, perhaps forever, the child to whom they are genetically connected. Subsequently, they undergo multiple losses associated with the loss of role, the loss of contact, and perhaps the loss of the other birth parent, which reshape the entire course of their lives.

Adoptees suffer their first loss at the initial separation from the birth family. Awareness of their adopted status is inevitable. Even if the loss is beyond conscious awareness, recognition, or vocabulary, it affects the adoptee on a very profound level. Any subsequent loss, or the perceived threat of separation, becomes more formidable for adoptees than their non-adopted peers.

The losses in adoption and the role they play in all triad members' lives have largely been ignored. The grief process in adoption, so necessary for healthy functioning, is further complicated by the fact that there is no end to the losses, no closure to the loss experience. Loss in adoption is not a single occurrence. There is the initial, identifiable loss and innumerable secondary sub-losses. Loss becomes an evolving process, creating a theme of loss in both the individual's and family's development. Those losses affect all subsequent development.

Loss is always a part of triad members' lives. A loss in adoption is never totally forgotten. It remains either in conscious awareness or is pushed into the unconscious, only to be reawakened by later loss. It is crucial for triad members, their significant others, and the professional with whom they interface, to recognize these losses and the effect loss has on their lives.

Rejection

Feelings of loss are exacerbated by keen feelings of rejection. One way individuals seek to cope with a loss is to personalize it. Triad members attempt to decipher what they did or did not do that led to the loss. Triad members become sensitive to the slightest hint of rejection, causing them either to avoid situations where they might be rejected or to provoke rejection in order to validate their earlier negative self-perceptions.

Adoptees seldom are able to view their placement into adoption by the birthparents as anything other than total rejection. Adoptees even at young ages grasp the concept that to be "chosen" means first that one was "un-chosen," reinforcing adoptees' lowered self-concept. Society promulgates the idea that the "good" adoptee is the one who is not curious and accepts adoption without question. At the other extreme of the continuum is the "bad" adoptee who is constantly questioning, thereby creating feelings of rejection in the adoptive parents.

Birthparents frequently condemn themselves for being irresponsible, as does society. Adoptive parents may inadvertently create fantasies for the adoptee about the birth family, which reinforce these feelings of rejection. For example, adoptive parents may block an adolescent adoptee's interest in searching for birthparents by stating that the birthparents may have married and had other children. The implication is clear that the birthparents would consider contact with the adoptee an unwelcome intrusion.

Adoptive parents may sense that their bodies have rejected them if they are infertile. This impression may lead the infertile couple, for example, to feel betrayed or rejected by God. When they come to adoption, the adopters, possibly unconsciously, anticipate the birthparents' rejection and criticism of their parenting. Adoptive parents struggle with issues of entitlement, wondering if perhaps they were never meant to be parents, especially to this child. The adopting family, then, may watch for the adoptee to reject them, interpreting many benign, childish actions as rejection. To avoid that ultimate rejection, some adoptive parents expel or bind adolescent adoptees prior to the accomplishment of appropriate emancipation tasks.

Guilt/Shame

The sense of deserving such rejection leads triad members to experience tremendous guilt and shame. They commonly believe that there is something intrinsically wrong with them or their deeds that caused the losses to occur. Most triad members have internalized, romantic images of the American family that remain unfulfilled because there is no positive, realistic view of the adoptive family in our society.

For many triad members, the shame of being involved in adoption per se exists passively, often without recognition. The shame of an unplanned pregnancy, or the crisis of infertility, or the shame of having been given up remains unspoken, often as an unconscious motivator.

Adoptees suggest that something about their very being caused the adoption. The self-accusation is intensified by the secrecy often present in past and present adoption practices. These factors combine to lead the adoptee to conclude that the feelings of guilt and shame are indeed valid.

Adoptive parents, when they are diagnosed as infertile, frequently believe that they must have committed a grave sin to receive such a harsh sentence. They are ashamed of themselves, of their defective bodies, of their inability to bear children.

Birthparents feel tremendous guilt and shame for having been intimate and sexual; for the very act of conception, they find themselves guilty.

Grief

Every loss in adoption must be grieved. The losses in adoption, however, are difficult to mourn in a society where adoption is seen as a problem-solving event filled with joy. There are no rituals to bury the unborn children; no rites to mark off the loss of role of caretaking parents; no ceremonies for lost dreams or unknown families. Grief washes over triad members' lives, particularly at times of subsequent loss or developmental transitions.

Triad members can be assisted at any point in the adoption experience by learning about and discussing the five stages of grief: denial, anger, bargaining, depression, and acceptance (Kubler-Ross 1969).

Adoptees in their youth find it difficult to grieve their losses, although they are in many instances aware of them, even as young children. Youngsters removed from abusive homes are expected to feel only relief and gratitude, not loss and grief. Adults block children's expressions of pain or attempt to divert them. In addition, due to developmental unfolding of cognitive processes, adoptees do not fully appreciate the total impact of their losses into their adolescence or, for many, into adulthood. This delayed grief may lead to depression or acting out through substance abuse or aggressive behaviors.

Birthparents may undergo an initial, brief, intense period of grief at the time of the loss of the child, but are encouraged by well-meaning friends and family to move on in their lives and to believe that their child is better off. The grief, however, does not vanish, and, in fact, it has been reported that birth mothers may deny the experience for up to ten years (Campbell 1979).

Family and friends, who encourage the couple to adopt, as if children are interchangeable, also block adoptive parents' grief over the inability to bear children. The grief of the adoptive parents continues as the child grows up since the adoptee can never fully meet the fantasies and expectations of the adoptive parents.

Identity

Adoption may also threaten triad members' sense of identity. Triad members often express feelings related to confused identity and identity crises, particularly at times of unrelated loss.

Identity is defined both by what one is and what one is not. In adoption, birthparents are parents and are not. Adoptive parents who were not parents suddenly become parents. Adoptees born into one family, a family probably nameless to them now, lose an identity and then borrow one from the adopting family.

Adoption, for some, precludes a complete or integrated sense of self. Triad members may experience themselves as incomplete, deficient, or unfinished. They state that they lack feelings of well-being, integration, or solidity associated with a fully developed identity.

Adoptees lacking medical, genetic, religious, and historical information are plagued by questions such as: Who are they? Why were they born? Were they in fact merely a mistake, not meant to have been born, an accident? This lack of identity may lead adoptees, particularly in adolescent years, to seek out ways to belong in more extreme fashion than many of their non-adopted peers. Adolescent adoptees are over represented among those who join sub-cultures, run away, become pregnant, or totally reject their families.

For many couples in our society a sense of identity is tied to procreation. Adoptive parents may lose that sense of generativity, of being fled to the past and future, often created through procreation.

Adoptive parents and birthparents share a common experience of role confusion. They are handicapped by the lack of positive identity associated with being either a birthparent or adoptive parent (Kirk 1964). Neither set of parents can lay full claim to the adoptee nor can they gain distance from any problems that may arise.

Intimacy

The multiple, ongoing losses in adoption, coupled with feelings of rejection, shame, and grief as well as an incomplete sense of self, may impede the development of intimacy for triad members. One maladaptive way to avoid possible reenactment of previous losses is to avoid closeness and commitment.

Adoptive parents report that their adopted children seem to hold back a part of themselves in the relationship. Adoptive mothers indicate, for example, that even as an infant, the adoptee was "not cuddly." Many adoptees as teens state that they truly have never felt close to anyone. Some youngsters declare lifetime emptiness related to a longing for the birthmother they may have never seen.

Due to these multiple losses for both adoptees and adoptive parents, there may also have been difficulties in early bonding and attachment. For children adopted at older ages, multiple disruptions in attachment and/or abuse may interfere with relationships in the new family (Fahlberg 1979 a,b).

The adoptee's intimacy issues are particularly evident in relationships with members of the opposite sex and revolve around questions about the adoptee's conception, biological and genetic concerns, and sexuality.

The adoptive parents' couple relationship may have been irreparably harmed by the intrusive nature of medical procedures and the scapegoating and blame that may have been part of the diagnosis of infertility. These residual effects may become the hallmark of the later relationship.

Birthparents may come to equate sex, intimacy, and pregnancy with pain leading them to avoid additional loss by shunning intimate relationships. Further, birthparents may question their ability to parent a child successfully. In many instances, the birthparents fear intimacy in relationships with opposite sex partners, family or subsequent children.

Mastery/Control

Adoption alters the course of one's life. This shift presents triad members with additional hurdles in their development, and may hinder growth, self-actualization, and the evolution of self-control.

Birthparents, adoptive parents, and adoptees are all forced to give up control. Adoption, for most, is a second choice. Birthparents did not grow up with romantic images of becoming accidentally pregnant or abusing their children and surrendering them for adoption. In contrast, the pregnancy or abuse is a crisis situation whose resolution becomes adoption. In order to solve the predicament, birthparents must surrender not only the child but also their volition, leading to feelings of victimization and powerlessness, which may become themes in birthparents' lives.

Adoptees are keenly aware that they were not party to the decision which led to their adoption. They had no control over the loss of the birth family or the choice of the adoptive family. The adoption proceeded with adults making life-altering choices for them. This unnatural change of course impinges on growth toward self-actualization and self-control. Adolescent adoptees, attempting to master the loss of control they have experienced in adoption, frequently engage in power struggles with adoptive parents and other authority figures. They may lack internalized self-control, leading to a lowered sense of self-responsibility. These patterns, frequently passive/aggressive in nature, may continue into adulthood.

For adoptive parents, the intricacies of the adoption process lead to feelings of helplessness. These feelings sometimes cause adoptive parents to view themselves as powerless, and perhaps entitled to be parents, leading to laxity in parenting. As an alternative response, some adoptive parents may seek to regain the lost control by becoming overprotective and controlling, leading to rigidity in the parent/adoptee relationship.

Summary

The experience of adoption, then, can be one of loss, rejection, guilt/shame, grief, diminished identity, thwarted intimacy, and threats to self-control and to the accomplishment of mastery. These seven core or lifelong issues permeate the lives of triad members regardless of the circumstances of the adoption.

Identifying these core issues can assist triad members and professionals in establishing an open dialogue and alleviating some of the pain and isolation, which so often characterize adoption. Triad members may need professional assistance in recognizing that they may have become trapped in the negative feelings generated by the adoption experience. Armed with this new awareness, they can choose to catapult themselves into growth and strength.

Triad members may repeatedly do and undo their adoption experiences in their minds and in their vacillating behaviors while striving toward mastery. They will benefit from identifying, exploring and ultimately accepting the role of the seven core issues in their lives.

The following tasks and questions will help triad members and professionals explore the seven core issues in adoption:

- List the losses, large and small, that you have experienced in adoption.
- Identify the feelings associated with these losses.
- What experiences in adoption have led to feelings of rejection?
- Do you ever see yourself rejecting others before they can reject you? When?
- What guilt or shame do you feel about adoption?
- What feelings do you experience when you talk about adoption?
- Identify your behaviors at each of the five stages of the grief process. Have you accepted your losses?
- How has adoption impacted your sense of who you are?

This article originally appeared on Deborah Silverstein and Shanon Kaplan's website, www.adopting.org . It is reprinted with permission of the authors.

grief & loss

WE ASSUME A CRITICAL TASK
WHEN WE SEEK TO HELP
MOURNING CHILDREN. OUR
SUCCESS DEPENDS ON OUR
WILLINGNESS TO OFFER
SUPPORT DURING A TROUBLED
AND BAFFLING TIME.
                    – Claudia L. Jewitt

Loss and Grief in Adoption

by Marlou Russell, Ph.D.

Loss is an inherent part of adoption. In adoption, adoptees lose their birth families, birth parents lose their children, and adoptive parents lose their dream of the child they originally wanted to have. The structure of adoption is such that to create an adoptive family a birth family must be separated.

Special needs adoption adds another layer of loss to adoption. The loss of health, siblings, cultural familiarity and caretakers will affect the adoptee. The adoptee's losses are then passed on to the adoptive parents and birth parents via tentative and precarious relationships.

Unless loss is recognized, grieving cannot take place. Oftentimes when an adoption is finalized, triad members are focusing on the next phase of their lives—the adoptive parents are busy raising their child, the birth parents are attempting to move on in their lives, and the adoptee is getting used to new caretakers.

Recognizing the stages of grief can reassure triad members that they are experiencing appropriate feelings. Adults, children, and even infants can show the signs and symptoms of loss and grief. When the losses of adoption are addressed, the gains of adoption can be more fully appreciated.

Kubler-Ross Stages of Grief

Elisabeth Kubler-Ross has been a pioneer in the field of death and dying research. In her work with dying people and those close to them, she has identified five stages of the normal grieving process. These five stages can be worked through in any order. Some stages may be revisited, but typically people pass through all five stages in their processing of grief issues.

Denial

The first stage of grieving is denial. Feeling shock, disbelief, numb, and detached is common. The incident or feelings are kept out of one's awareness. Denial is protective in that it helps people to function when the truth or clarity would be too much to handle. Staying in denial, however, has negative consequences. To ignore important issues and feelings is like having a pink elephant in the living room that no one talks about. Everyone walks around it and pretends it isn't there even though it's in the way of everything.

Anger
The second stage of grieving is anger. Anger is the feeling that a situation is unfair and should not have happened. It is common in the anger stage to look for someone to blame. Anger can also be very motivating and inspire one to take action. The anger stage can help a person make changes in their life. Many worthwhile organizations have grown out of the energy that anger can produce.

Bargaining
The third stage of grieving is bargaining. Bargaining involves trying to find ways to undo the situation by searching for trade-offs. Being in the stage of bargaining means that the person is no longer in denial. There is a real awareness of the loss, and the bargaining is an attempt to control a situation that feels out of control.

Depression
The fourth stage of grieving is depression. Feelings of helplessness and hopelessness can be present as well as a lack of energy, changes in eating or sleeping patterns, irritability, lack of interest in usual activities, sadness, and an inability to concentrate.

Acceptance
The fifth and final stage of grieving is acceptance. The loss is no longer the main focus and there is room for other activities and interests. The goal of acceptance in adoption is not to forget the person or that an adoption has taken place. That would bring one back to the stage of denial. The goal of acceptance is to honour and integrate the people and experience of adoption.

Grieving in Adoption
Grieving in adoption is different in some distinct ways from mourning the death of someone who has died. When someone dies, there is a definite ending that allows grieving to begin. In adoption, there is no death, no ending. In adoption, a state of limbo exists that is similar to the dynamics of mourning someone who is missing in action. It is difficult to mourn someone who is alive but unavailable.

It is important to acknowledge and address the phases of grieving as they appear. Events and situations in each triad member's life will trigger feelings of adoption loss. Acknowledging and expressing these feelings appropriately allows the grieving process to proceed and healing to take place.

Feelings of loss and the need to grieve can occur despite the level of contact and communication between triad members. Adoptees can miss their birth parents or former caretakers even if there was abuse. Birth parents can miss their children regardless of the circumstances of the separation. Adoptive parents can miss the simpler life they had before the adoption.

Adoption triad members need to be aware of the issues of adoption and be around people who understand the complexities of adoption. Conferences, books, and the Internet are a great source of information on all aspects of the adoption experience. Adoption support groups offer camaraderie, validation, and practical information.

The losses of adoption cannot be avoided. However, the process of grieving and reaching out to others for support can provide emotional relief and the knowledge that you are not alone on your journey of adoption.

This article originally appeared in the SNAP newsletter, Vol. 16 #3, Fall 2000. It is reprinted here by permission of the author.

Grief & Loss in Adopted Children

by Lissa Cowan

How Does Loss Affect the Adopted Child?

The ramifications of loss on adopted children can be devastating. If not resolved at an early age this emotional distress can lead to depression, attachment issues, substance abuse, and suicidal tendencies.

Unlike the death of a loved one, it is difficult for a child to mourn the loss of a parent when little is known about the reasons for placing the child. Many questions accompany these feelings of loss such as: did the parents die or separate, were they unable to keep the child due to poverty, illness or abuse? If the child is from another country, were they victims of wartime?

When children are adopted they feel a heightened sense of vulnerability. They often experience feelings of futility, and a loss of self-esteem. Questions like "Who will keep me safe?" often run through the child's mind. In John Bowlby's three-volume work called *Attachment and Loss* he writes that children grieve as deeply as their elders. Bowlby teaches us that just because children don't have the same concerns and issues as adults, doesn't mean their emotions are any less complex. Understanding and acknowledging this reality is a vital step toward giving children who are adopted the understanding, support and attention they need to work through the grieving process.

When an adult experiences a loss, either through death, adoption or divorce, his or her world is reduced. As a child or adolescent, this experience is compounded because there is often a greater sense of being disoriented and alone in the world. In her book entitled *Beyond Grief*, Carol Staudacher uses the words "locate myself" to refer to what a child is trying to do when it experiences a loss. Though, no matter how intense, the child wouldn't verbalize these feelings.

The following is a list of fears resulting from loss during childhood. Although these fears relate to the death of a loved one, there are many similarities to the loss felt by a child who is adopted.

Fear of losing the other parent
If death or an adoption has removed a parent from a child's life, the child may see the remaining parent as a candidate for a similar fate.

Fear of going to sleep
A child may be afraid of going to sleep because he or she equates sleep with loss or death. Also, sleep can separate the people in the home from the child who is sent to bed while the activity in other rooms continues. The awake, mobile family can desert the sleeping child who is in the dark in an isolated environment.

Fear of being separated from the parent or sibling
The child may fear being left with a baby sitter or being required to go some place unaccompanied by an older brother or sister. The fear of separation can be drastic and long-lasting for the child who has experienced a loss.

Fear of being unprotected
Because the child feels that he or she has been deserted there is a feeling of being no longer protected. For a young child this can be quite terrifying.

Fear of sharing his or her feelings with others
The fear of sharing one's feeling is often stronger in the adolescent. If the adolescent shares his or her feelings the status quo may be upset. A family member may not understand and may have an opposite reaction to the child wishing to share his or her feelings. Often children keep their feelings to themselves for fear of hurting a family member (Staudacher, 1987).

Supporting The Adopted Child's Feelings Of Loss

The way parents and caretakers respond to a child's feelings of loss is a critical factor for how well the loss is eventually resolved. It is important that parents accept and listen to the child's feelings, even though they may not necessarily correspond to their own feelings at the time. Saying things like "You shouldn't feel that way" or "That's not the way it is at all" undervalues the child's emotional state and sets back the child's process of healing.

Similarly, when a child is in the process of a move to another family, it is not good to boost the child's hopes by saying things like, "They'll keep you forever," or "You'll love it there." Because the child is grieving, he or she may not love it there at all. It is important at this point to allow the child the freedom to grieve, otherwise these feelings won't have anywhere to go and will remain bottled up. If adoptive or foster parents urge the child not to dwell in the past, this may cut off an opportunity for the child to share his or her feelings. These emotions will then remain tied to the past and the child's energies will in turn stay tied to the loved one, meaning that other areas of living will be impeded.

Strategies to Help A Child Heal

In *Helping Children Cope with Separation and Loss,* Claudia L. Jewitt gives examples of strategies to help the adopted child feel validated. The following strategy features a special needs child who was adopted from another country, and how the parent dealt with the question of the child's past, and his or her birth parents.

Most adopted kids sometimes think about their birth parents. You might wonder what they were like and why they didn't take care of you until you were grown up. No one really knows about your parents; none of us got to talk to them, so we can only guess. But I'll tell you why this happens to a lot of other kids in your birth country. It happens because there isn't enough money, or food. Or the family doesn't think they can give the child a good life. Or there is a war and people get killed. Or the child is of a different race and no one will help the mother. My best guess is that your parents' reason was one of these. What I'm sure about is that they didn't leave you because you did something bad or because you weren't lovable.

Often adopted children may feel conflicting loyalties. They may think that they are expected to give up the memory of the birth parents or of a previous caretaker. Claudia L. Jewitt writes that it is important to let the child know that quite the opposite is true. She writes, "the more distinct the two relationships are kept, the more the new one is likely to prosper." She suggests the ritual of lighting candles to honour the child's feelings for both sets of parents or caretakers. The purpose of this ritual is to give the child permission to get close to a new caretaker while still valuing the closeness he or she feels for previous ones.

Holding one candle you might say, "When you were born, you had the gift to give love and get love. This gift is like a light; it makes me feel warm and happy" (then you light the candle representing the child). "Your mom cuddled and fed you and you felt close to her" (put the child's candle next to the unlit candle representing the mom until it lights). "Your dad thought you were special. He played with you, and so on" (then light the third candle representing the father with the child's candle). After this is done, the child can light candles symbolizing the present parents or caretakers who may wish to add that the love the child feels for his or her birthparents or previous caretakers will never go out.

New Beginnings, Old Yearnings

"But isn't adoption supposed to be a happy time—a new beginning?" Dianne Harrison asks this question in "Understanding the Grief of Adopted Children", taken from *Growing Together*, (Vol. 1, No. 10, August 1986). She says it's important to remember that in adoption "a process of understanding the past, grieving for it, and then letting it go must be complete before our children can move forward." Harrison suggests becoming familiar with Kubler-Ross' stages of grief to better understand what feelings the child is going through. Sometimes the stages might overlap depending on what the child experienced during early development, but it will still give you a sense of where they're at.

According to Anna Freud, "healthy mourning" happens when changes in the external sphere of life are accepted and brought into the internal sphere of life. This acceptance is needed for the adopted child to feel attachment again. However, "change" doesn't happen overnight. Because it is a long process of understanding, it is important to take one day at a time. This can be difficult when the pain and frustration you see your child undergo seem never-ending.

When children resolve grief issues the self-esteem damaged by the loss is eventually restored (Jewitt, 1982). And, although the yearning never goes away, some may feel that their loss has given them a new appreciation of life.

This article originally appeared in the SNAP newsletter, Vol. 16, #3, fall 2000. © 2000 Society of Special Needs Adoptive Parents.

But What About Sadness?

An Adoptive Parent's Perspective

by Ro de Bree

Before May of 1993, our lives were relatively easy. No home full of teenage boys is problem-free, but we thought we were either managing pretty well or luckier than most. In spite of minor glitches, usually engineered by our third son, all the boys seemed to be coping. Our youngest, previously diagnosed with Fetal Alcohol Syndrome, was compliant, successful at school, and popular. While his diagnosis of permanent brain damage had been frightening at first, we now thought his impairment minimal, and predictions regarding his future grossly exaggerated.

Before May of 1993, I would have described myself as casual and easy-going, happy and contented, a good mother, a person with no major anxieties.

Four months later, at the end of September, I was tense and nervous, anxiously questioning my parenting skills, overwhelmed with guilt, isolating myself, unable to sleep, and anorexic. "It's the shock," said family and friends, as my hair turned white, almost overnight.

Our third son, source of all these new problems, was by then tucked away in a youth detention centre, and in the opinion of family and friends, it was "the best thing that could have happened. He's learned his lesson, and now he'll start to behave himself."

But he wasn't able to learn from his mistakes. Instead, he learned survival skills: how to survive in Juvie, in a group home, in adult jails, on the streets.... He learned how to manage comfortably in the legal system and Corrections; he learned to manipulate Social Services.

My youngest, leaving home two years later, learned different lessons: how to gain attention through suicide attempts and other major medical problems, how to manipulate the health care system to his advantage, and how to best avoid the responsibilities of being a father.

I learned to support, to defend, to advocate. I learned to live with constant, unrelieved stress. As yet another devastating diagnosis of FAS was thrust upon us, I learned what those three letters really stand for. I learned the beginnings of the grieving process.

Special Needs, Special Losses

Grief is a normal response to loss. Parents of any child with a disability mourn the loss of dreams and hopes for their child, the loss of normal development, the loss of potential and the loss of future relationships.

But those of us who choose to adopt special needs children with FAS are parenting some of the most difficult, most unique, most challenging children in British Columbia, and we mourn other losses, too.

Adoptive parents, who have been "approved" for parenting, have very high expectations of themselves—asking for help is really hard. When we finally reach the level of acute desperation and start searching, we find that there are very few knowledgeable professionals out there, very few sustainable services for little kids, and absolutely nothing for non-compliant teens with FAS. We grieve the lack of necessary, on-going assistance for our children.

We aren't the only parents coping with FAS, but we often feel alone when it comes down to bottom lines. Sometimes we must choose to parent our children outside of our household. When this happens, the foster parents or group home leaders who share our parenting don't share either our love or our grief. Birth parents, living with their own FAS children, often share our guilt issues but usually avoid the devastation of attachment disorder. Having finally bonded with our children, we now grieve the loss of emotional closeness.

I also mourn losses in my sons' health. A few months ago, one of them finished off a drunken brawl with a perforated bowel, followed by acute peritonitis. Early addictions have already led to damage being dealt out by drug dealers; early sexual exploits have led to unpleasant diseases. Medications have been abused, and broken bones have been neglected. Many missed dental appointments have finally resulted in pulled teeth.

For my husband, who comes from a cultural background that emphasized the importance of a "good name," the loss of his good reputation—the direct result of having a child's crime spread across the front page of the local paper— was an enormous source of grief. And he found the loss of privacy, especially in relation to the Youth Justice System, even harder to bear.

And, as our homes become war zones, adoptive parents of FAS-affected kids mourn smaller losses: the continued lack of understanding in our extended families, the loss of our own social networks as we run out of energy and lose the knack of having fun, and the struggle, during holidays and birthdays, to maintain some semblance of normalcy and tradition as our lives fall apart around us.

Grieving Without Closure

The "Stages of Grief," first expressed by Elizabeth Kubler-Ross and later modified by other experts, don't always seem to connect with the experiences of those who grieve without closure. Very often, parents of children with FAS don't even know a grieving process has started. As I interacted with the now near-strangers who, before my son entered the youth criminal subculture, had been my closest family, "anxiety" or even "panic" would have seemed a more accurate description of my emotional state that "grief."

Most parents, facing the challenges— and at first the denials within themselves of a child's permanent physical disability—are often still dealing with a diagnosis of a very young child. They grieve, but at least they also *know* early on.

Diagnosis of neurological damage commonly happens with much older children, especially in the adoption community. When our youngest, then fourteen, tested positive for FAS, relief dominated. Anxiety and guilt followed closely, but denial, another of the stages of grief, wasn't a necessary alternative. After all, my third son was almost old enough to leave the nest anyway, when he became an active participant in the Legal System. Corrections sent him to Burnaby for assessment; I heard his diagnosis in court when it was presented to the Judge. Denial would have been a tad redundant at that point.

When we finally had the whole picture—three of our children have alcohol related birth defects—the time for early intervention was past and the windows of opportunity were closed. But my whole life seemed to be taken up with the guilt of not knowing earlier, of not helping more, of not creating change. For me, guilt has always been one of the hardest stages of grief.

But anger has been a breeze. There seemed to be no point in wasting energy being angry at a birth mother who didn't understand, at adoption services with no knowledge, or at a son who had already left home before he got started on a life of crime. I couldn't blame the courts for my son's sentences, or the jails for his continuing incarcerations. Drug and alcohol addictions, suicide attempts, and my other son abandoning his baby daughter became, for me, places of guilt because of my boys' actions, rather than places of outrage. My counsellor says the anger is there: she says anger turned inwards becomes depression.

What About Sadness?

Acceptance of my children's neurological damage happened quite quickly. Acceptance of their dysfunctional social circles, unusual life style choices, very limited financial skills, and the fact that our relationships will always have to be parent/teenager rather than adult/adult, has come with time. But acceptance of their behaviours will always be difficult. As crisis follows crisis and I watch the deteriorations in their health, reasoning abilities, judgments, choices, and job opportunities, my grieving process, like a treadmill, goes around again.

It seems that I, along with others in our special needs adoptive parents support group, am unable to complete the "Stages of Grief." For some, acceptance is a problem, for others, denial is a major issue. Some of us are struck in anger. For me the missing step is still sadness.

FAS parents are good at adjusting: after every crisis, there has to be another adjustment to a new reality. Unfortunately, the crises in our lives are on going, because our children's issues never seem to finish off. We see a slow process of disintegration, but we seldom see improvements. And also we aren't very good at grieving our children's losses. We circle onwards; we never come to closure.

This article originally appeared in the SNAP newsletter, Vol. 15 #2, summer 1999. © 1999 Society of Special Needs Adoptive Parents.

attachment

RAISING A KID WITH REACTIVE
ATTACHMENT DISORDER IS A
BUMMER. THE "LOVING" PART IS
EASY, THE "LIKING" PART IS VERY
HARD, AND THE "PARENTING"
PART IS NOT FAIR!
— A Mother

Attachment:

A Core Issue in Special Needs Adoption

by Sara Graefe

Attachment is undoubtedly one of the top issues affecting families who access services here at SNAP.

What is Attachment?

Attachment has been defined as a "lasting psychological connectedness between human beings" (Bowlby, 1969), "an affectionate bond between two individuals that endures through space and time and serves to join them emotionally" (Kennell, 1976).

Humans are social beings. The ability to attach allows us to form and maintain affectionate ties and meaningful relationships with others throughout our lifetime.

The terms "bonding" and "attachment" are often used interchangeably. In recent years some experts have tried to separate the two concepts, using bonding to define the unique tie between the child and birth mother that occurs as a result of the shared physical experience during pregnancy and birth (Bourguignon & Watson, 1987).

Attachment, on the other hand, is a learned behaviour that begins shortly after birth and continues naturally for the first two to three years of life. Attachment develops out of a sequence of reciprocal interactions between the baby and the primary caregiver(s) as they learn about each other. An interaction is "reciprocal" when both caregiver and baby are responding to some cue from the other—such as when the baby smiles and the caregiver smiles back (or vice versa), when the baby looks into the caregiver's eyes and the caregiver gazes back, or when the baby cries out of discomfort and the caregiver responds by picking the baby up, soothing, cuddling, talking, and doing something to comfort the baby and meet their needs (e.g. feeding, changing, etc.) In the latter example, the baby reciprocally responds to the primary caregiver by calming down—and thus, begins to experience that caregivers can be trusted and that people will meet his/her needs.

When these interactions are repeated thousands of times during the first years of a baby's life, and the primary caregiver responds to the baby's needs the majority of the time, a secure sense of attachment develops. The young child develops the belief that others can be trusted, that those who love them are likely to try to help them and eliminate their discomfort and pain, and that the world is basically a safe place to be.

Attachment and Adoption

In our experience at SNAP, attachment issues impact most adoptees on some level. All adopted people share the loss of the birth mother—the person with whom they experienced that first, crucial physical bond during gestation and birth—and must face the tremendous grief that comes along with that.

For many of our kids, the attachment/bonding cycle during those critical early stages of life was further (and seriously) interrupted due to any number of factors, including difficult pregnancy and birth, the birth mom's substance abuse during pregnancy, maternal stress or trauma, separations from primary caregivers, abuse, neglect, inappropriate foster care and multiple foster placements before adoption. Typically, these children do not learn to trust. They become oppositional, angry, and often dangerous to themselves and others. Many of them suffer from attachment disorder, which has been described as "one of the most difficult emotional and behavioural conditions" (Pickle, 1997).

Reactive Attachment Disorder

Attachment Disorder (AD)—or Reactive Attachment Disorder (RAD) as it is officially called in the American Psychiatric Association's *Diagnostic and Statistics Manual*—is the inability to form normal relationships with others, and an impairment in development. Common symptoms of RAD include:

Emotional
- inability to give and receive genuine affection
- indiscriminate, superficial affection with strangers
- inappropriately demanding or clingy
- marked control problems; extreme defiance and anger

Social
- poor peer relationships
- poor eye contact; lack of eye contact on parental terms
- manipulative; superficially engaging and charming
- engages in persistent nonsense questions or incessant chatter
- fights for control over everything
- lacks understanding of social cues; lacks empathy

Behavioural
- destructive to self, others, animals, material things; accident prone
- stealing
- chronic, nonsensical lying
- vandalism and destructiveness
- hoarding or gorging food
- preoccupation with fire or gore

Developmental
- developmental lags
- lack of impulse control, and of cause and effect thinking
- learning and speech disorders
- lack of conscience; no remorse

An accurate diagnosis of Reactive Attachment Disorder is important. If you think your child has an attachment disorder, assessment should be made by a trained professional.

This article originally appeared in the SNAP newsletter, Vol. 16 #2, summer 2000. © 2000 Society of Special Needs Adoptive Parents.

Trauma & Attachment
by Rebecca Perbix Mallos, MSW

As the adoption of special needs children rises in this country, so does the need for adequate post adoption services. The current condition of post adoption services in most states still reflects the old adage of "just give them enough love and they'll be fine." This was probably true during the last era of special needs adoptions, which was before World War II. Before that war, the average age of children being placed for adoption in the U.S. was 4 years old. Most of the children being placed then were available because their families were not able to financially care for them or because a single parent could not provide adequate resources. After World War II, the world of adoption changed with the dramatic increase in infants available for adoption. This trend lasted into the 1960s when adoption again began to change with the advent of birth control. Once again, older children came to dominate the landscape of adoption.

Trauma & Special Needs Adoption
Our current dilemma in older child adoption, now called special needs adoption, is the level of trauma children have experienced prior to placement. While

prenatal exposure to alcohol was a possibility before World War II, prenatal exposure to drugs was virtually non-existent. In addition, current special needs children, if not prenatally exposed, typically have lived in their original family where drugs and alcohol are the driving force behind the chaos, abuse and neglect these children suffer. The availability of relevant post-adoption services has not kept pace with the need to help families raising traumatized children. I have worked in social services and mental health for over 22 years and I cannot remember a child I have met who has not been exposed to a family setting that included drugs and alcohol. This may be due to the fact that I have worked in community mental health, domestic violence, foster care and post adoption, all areas in which children who have experienced trauma are likely to be seen.

Parents who have adopted children with special needs know that a child who has previously experienced trauma from having lived in chaos, abuse and neglect is affected in all of the child's functioning systems. The child's cognitive, emotional, behavioural and physical systems have all been impacted by early trauma. Consider how many of the following traumatic experiences your child has endured:
• Parental alcoholism
• Parental substance abuse
• Group care/out of home care
• Mental illness in parent(s)
• Sexual abuse
• Emotional abuse
• Physical abuse
• Neglect
• Poverty
• Abandonment
• Divorce
• Loss of family
• Malnutrition
• Physical illness
Our kids have suffered much trauma. My foster son experienced eleven things on this list before age eight.

Attachment & PTSD
Traditionally, mental health practitioners have diagnosed children with behavioural symptoms subsequent to trauma with diagnoses such as Reactive Attachment Disorder, Attention Deficit Disorder, Oppositional Defiant Disorder, Conduct Disorder, etc. These symptoms could also be called Post Traumatic

Stress Disorder (PTSD.) This is not to say that those first disorders do not exist—obviously they do. However, my question is, to what degree are the behavioral symptoms presented by a child symptoms of traumatic stress? If so, we then have a basis for understanding the symptom rather than simply the behavioral description the other diagnoses provide. For instance, is it possible that what has traditionally been called Attachment Disorder is more effectively called Post Traumatic Stress Disorder? A child experiences disorders in their ability to successfully attach because the trauma symptoms the child presents in the new family are based on the child's previous traumatic experiences and are not useful. I came to this way of thinking by many routes, one being through the research on adults with Post Traumatic Stress Disorder, primarily Vietnam War Veterans. This research describes how difficult it is for the family of the veteran with PTSD to live with the behavioral symptoms of the vet re-experiencing the trauma of the war on a daily basis. This does not necessarily mean flashbacks. It can mean mood swings; hyper vigilance, unpredictable anger, despair and a strong need to control every situation.

Trauma & Memory

Another way I understand the correlation of behavioral disorders to PTSD is the way in which trauma is stored in the brain. For instance, memories are encoded in the brain in different ways. Declarative memory contains facts—explicit details about events that can be verbalized. Non-declarative memory, or implicit memory, is experienced viscerally and is not immediately available for verbalization. Recent experiments with adult victims of trauma have shown that when an event is perceived to be traumatic, i.e. life threatening, that part of the brain that gives language to the experience stops working. Instead, the traumatic event gets stored in the sensory-motor domain of the brain. Another way to think about this is to understand that each of our brains has an extensive filing and storage system for details and experiences. Like all memory, traumatic memory gets stored too.

This is useful for us when we can make use of memory as a way to protect us from further trauma. It is helpful to be able to call out of memory that a particular situation is potentially threatening and our response needs to be protective. However, for those of us who have not experienced trauma as a daily event, we are selective in our understanding of what is threatening because we believe we are generally safe. Our special needs children do not have that advantage. Their experience has been that the world is a dangerous, threatening, hostile and uncaring place and that potential danger is always present. That means that the filing system in their brain is stored with memories that indicate that even seemingly benign situations can carry some hidden threat. When a person is responding to their environment out of fear of a potential threat, they become hyper vigilant, their heart rate is often higher than normal, even at rest, and their adrenaline system is always pumped up ready for "fight or flight."

This "fight or flight" phenomenon is evident in children who are often defensive, or ready to blame others, are in need of controlling each situation they encounter, are usually ready to fight back when there is nothing to fight about, or seem to "check out" and become non-responsive to any requests. Children who are suffering from some form of PTSD or traumatic stress are both emotionally and neurophysiologically "alert" to potential danger.

Re-Doing the Experience

What is very hard for both parents and professionals to understand is that simply telling the traumatized child that this new family will not hurt them in the ways they have been hurt before is not enough to change the filing system in the brain. The way the filing system got filled up was by experience with trauma and highly emotional situations. One way to change what the filing system has assigned to a particular situation is to re-do the situation emotionally.

There are many ways to re-do the emotional experience. But because traumatized children operate at a higher level of adrenaline functioning, the new emotional experience is going to have to be highly charged. Some of the ways to evoke new emotions therapeutically are through movement, art, music, drama and through holding therapy. This last intervention is the most controversial for many people. I use many different interventions in my work with children but the one that appears to make the most difference for the most shut down, controlling and angry kid I know is holding therapy.

Holding Therapy

There is much misunderstanding in the general population and in the professional world about what holding therapy is or isn't. In my practice with colleagues at the Attachment Center Northwest outside Seattle, what holding therapy *is not,* is violent or abusive. When seen on TV, the part of the therapy that is shown is the catharsis. It is dramatic. That is just a segment of what really goes on. Holding therapy is nudging, cajoling, challenging and for the most part *nurturing.* Holding therapy allows for re-experiencing of a traumatic event, within an emotionally charged situation but this time the outcome of the trauma is different. The child gets taken care of rather than neglected, comforted rather that abandoned. The child shares his rage, fear and grief with nurturing adults who are in control and keeping the child safe. Parents who are safe, trustworthy and predictable are the most significant part of the therapy because they comfort the child at a time when the child is most vulnerable. For the traumatized and neglected child, this comfort is a new experience because most children from chaotic backgrounds have learned to take care of themselves. They have not allowed themselves to be comforted or nurtured because they don't know how.

Finding a therapist who understands trauma is critical when seeking services for a child with a traumatic past. The family needs to be an integral part of the therapy. The resolution of trauma, decrease in trauma-based behavior and increase in ability to be vulnerable and nurtured is what will lead the attachment-disordered child to risk attachment.

There are two national organizations [in the US] that are available to refer families to therapists in their communities who understand trauma and/or attachment. Those organizations are: ATTACh, PO Box 665, Annandale, VA, USA 22003-0665, ph.703-914-3928, web: www.attach.org; the International Society for Traumatic Stress Studies, 60 Revere Drive, Suite 500, Northbrook, Illinois USA 60062, ph. (847) 480-9028.

Taking care of our traumatized children requires that we take good care of ourselves. Finding the right help is the first step.

This article originally appeared in *Hoofbeats: News from the Attachment Disorder Network*, May/June 2000. It is reprinted here with permission of the author.

Treatment of Attachment Disorder:
Conventional vs Intrusive Therapy?
by Ellen Halliday

In his book *Adoption Disruption: Risks, Responses*, Richard Barth outlines why conventional therapy fails with attachment-disordered (AD) children. Some of these reasons include: only the child is seen in conventional therapy; many therapists do not help the family change the child's environment; play therapies are often ineffectual; many therapists fail to recognize that marital distress may be due to the troubled adoption; etc. Ken Magid and Carole McKelvey in *High Risk: Children Without a Conscience* add: "There are many traditional therapies we could critique, but suffice it to say that all of them fall short when dealing with the true Trust Bandit" ("Trust Bandit" is their term for children with attachment disorder).

Tori De Angelis agrees, emphasizing that conventional treatments don't work with these youngsters (*KC Connections*, a newsletter of the Association for

Treatment and Training in the Attachment of Children). She quotes Nancy Colletta, Ph.D.: "Traditional therapy is predicated on the idea that a child can build trust with someone. But it became clear to me that these kids were unable to trust adults."

However, conventional methods are nevertheless a place to start. As Foster Cline points out in his own book, *Hope for High Risk and Rage Filled Children,* "Intrusive therapies should not be considered unless other more traditional methods have been attempted without good results by a competent therapist."

Holding Nurturing Therapy

What seems to have some success with severe cases of attachment disorder is holding therapy, which is also known as holding nurturing therapy. As Allred and Keck point out, there seems to be a fair amount of confusion and misinformation about holding therapy: "therapists have developed their own versions of this technique ... but most of them call it by the same name." Many caregivers have turned to this type of alternative therapy that emphasizes prolonged eye contact, cradling and nurturing touch to enhance the bond between the child and adoptive parents.

Understanding the Controversy

Some controversy surrounds holding therapy. Some professionals think it traumatizes the child and may even be abusive. Some believe it causes a "trauma bond." A trauma bond is a very close (but unhealthy) attachment with a person who has abused the child. It is postulated that holding therapy generates such huge amounts of anxiety for the child that a trauma bond forms.

However, tests for anxiety before and after treatment performed at the Attachment Center at Evergreen (ACE) showed anxiety levels were not increased after therapy and that, in fact, of 45% of children with significant levels of anxiety before the treatment, only 15% continued having significant levels of anxiety after treatment. The test did uncover, however, that anxiety is a significant problem for almost one-half of the children who attend treatment at ACE (Liz Randolph, MSN, Ph.D.).

While little research has been conducted on these methods (holding), those using them claim a high success rate. Nancy Thomas, a therapist, claims that 85% of the children she's helped treat attach healthily with their adoptive or foster parents, and go on to succeed in school, form stable relationships and acquire and stay in jobs.

It appears that only one quantitative study has been done on holding therapy. Robin Myerhoff, in her Ph.D. dissertation, found that twelve children who received the therapy at The Attachment Center at Evergreen scored somewhat lower on aggression and delinquency after treatment. Eleven children who did not receive treatment showed no change.

Deborah Hage, MSW says the success rate of holding therapy depends on how soon parents utilize it, how disturbed the child is, the age of the child, and the parents' energy level during treatment (as it is very parent intensive). Holding therapy involves a commitment to the child above and beyond what traditional therapies require.

Terry M. Levy, Ph.D., who practices at Evergreen, says "holding techniques" have been controversial for many years. Some of the criticisms and misconceptions include: it is coercive, forces the child into submission, re-traumatizes, creates a trauma bond, interferes with bodily functions such as respiration and movement, brainwashes, degrades, is based on a rage reduction model, victimizes abused children, and is not proven effective. He says some of these criticisms were valid regarding the way certain practitioners utilized holding methods in the past. Certainly, the recent death of a ten year old adopted girl while undergoing rebirthing therapy at the renowned attachment clinic, Connell Watkins & Associates in Evergreen, Colorado, has refuelled the ongoing controversy over intrusive attachment therapies.

However, as Hage writes (ATTACh newsletter): "Holding therapies have been greatly misunderstood, sometimes misused, and often debated. Much of the debate focuses on whether holding a child close, in and of itself, is harmful or beneficial. Many therapists maintain it is beneficial." She goes on to say: "Parents in desperate straits seek effective measures. Most of the time, the more benign therapies are very efficacious. However, after other therapists have done everything in their power to make a change in the child's life, many parents choose to call a holding therapist."

"The most significant aspect of holding is what occurs after the rage/grief/fear are spent: the child, in a state of total relaxation, is able to accept, often for the first time, the love and concern of others." The child is receptive and at this point, "... the child and the parents then build on the child's receptivity to enter into a trusting relationship and employ additional methods based on behavioural and cognitive theories."

Terry M. Levy adds: "The 'Holding Nurturing Practice' [as it is known at Evergreen Attachment Center] is a powerful and effective therapeutic framework when used as part of the treatment for attachment disorder. There are, however, several concerns and contraindications. Specialized training and supervision is mandatory. Male-female co-therapists, within the context of a multidisciplinary treatment team, are most effective. Selecting the clinicians is important, as not all therapists feel comfortable with this approach. Countertransference issues are easily provoked, and these emotional reactions will inhibit therapeutic progress. Proper candidates must be selected. HNP is only used when conventional therapeutic approaches have been unsuccessful."

How Holding Therapy Works

The Attachment Centre at Evergreen in Colorado, where the HNP is practiced, is reputedly on the leading edge of holding therapy practice. The Evergreen Centre works mainly with children who are severe in their pathology.

At Evergreen, each child and family is assessed, and therapeutic and parenting techniques are designed around their needs. Rather than focusing on the generation and expression of anger, the most prominent emotion is worked with instead. However, rarely do the three emotions—fear, anger and sadness—not play a part.

In HNP, the therapist first cradles the child in their arms, and "social releasors" such as eye contact, smile, gentle firm touch, gentle movement, stimulation and soothing activate attachment behaviours. Holding therapy is designed to gain access to the infant brain or "old brain" which regulates attachment behaviour, and modifies deeply held infant beliefs and convictions. Secure attachment is more likely to be activated and can then be transferred to the parent-child relationship. It reduces the effect of severe and chronic stress (Levy, T.M.), a frequent state for these children who often suffer from post-traumatic stress disorder. The alarm system (triggering release of stress hormones) occurs too frequently in these children. HNP reduces the effect of severe and chronic stress, and reduces release of stress-induced hormones while facilitating the connection with the child and initiating the bonding process.

HNP also provides a relationship context in which the therapist can help the child learn to manage and modulate his or her own internal reactions. The therapist is in a position of authority, yet the child is safe. For example, a child can be safely held in arms through a temper tantrum, learning to talk about anger and frustration as an effective coping skill. These children often fear their own angry and aggressive impulses, and are afraid of hurting others and themselves. HNP provides a firm, yet nurturing, context, where children feel safe and secure and realize they will not do damage.

HNP also allows children to transcend chronic defences and avoids reinforcing negative behaviour patterns. Corrective and healing emotional experiences take place in a number of areas. New and more pro-social behaviours are learned. The development of new belief systems is encouraged.

Many attachment-disordered children have been sexually and physically abused, and are afraid of closeness and touch. They can learn the difference between bad touch and healthy touch, and learn to accept gentle, loving, nurturing closeness and touch.

The course of treatment at Evergreen takes place over ten consecutive days, three to four hours per day, with two therapists who try to work equally with the child, the parents, and perhaps other members of the family. The referring therapist is encouraged to attend as well.

The first part of the treatment educates the parents about attachment-disordered children. The second teaches the parents consequential parenting skills (i.e., how to provide corrective parenting experiences for the child). Third is intensive emotional work with the child, the goal being to help the child bond to the parents by assisting the child to regress to the period that produced the pathology in order to resolve old destructive emotions and create new bonds with their parents.

Three contracting parties are involved. Parents and child, therapist and child, and parents and therapist. The child is given the choice throughout the therapy of facing the consequences of their behaviour or going through the difficult work to resolve them, and the child is made to acknowledge the problems that brought the family to treatment.

Other Techniques

Therapy at the Evergreen Center and other locations where holding therapy is practiced may involve the use of a variety of techniques such as reparenting, inner child work, cognitive restructuring, EMDR, and therapeutic foster parenting, as well as the holding therapy.

EMDR

EMDR stands for "eye movement desensitization and reprocessing." EMDR is a therapeutic procedure in which rapid eye movements are induced while the individual focuses on a disturbing memory, feeling, image or body sensation associated with a past traumatic event or a current disturbing issue. The process accesses repressed memories and feelings, which the person has not previously been able to discuss or recall. People not only access and work through traumatic memories, but also integrate new, more positive concepts. The initial focus of EMDR was post-traumatic stress disorders. There are theoretical concepts of AD as a type of PTSD. The Attachment Center at Minnesota has found it possible to conclude from over two and a half years of using EMDR that it provides a mechanism for shifting "frozen conclusions," and the Center incorporates it into all phases of treatment.

Neurofeedback

Neurofeedback (also called EEG biofeedback or brainwave training) is a process of operant conditioning through which the trainee is able to slowly and cumulatively alter the patterns of the brain's bioelectrical activity, as reflected in the EEG. Fisher says the changes are often, even routinely, dramatic. Fisher goes on to say: "AD is the manifestation of brain damage to the right hemisphere. It is thought that Neurofeedback can…remediate the damage by helping to forge new neural pathways and calm the limbic brain." As noted earlier, kids with AD can live in almost constant flight or fight. Training the brain toward motor stillness seems to have a profoundly stabilizing effect. (Neurofeedback Treatment for Reactive Attachment Disorder Fisher, S.F., M.A.)

Neurodevelopmental Therapy, also used at the Evergreen Center, involves the implementation of specific activities or exercises designed to stimulate various areas of the brain. One of these is SAMONAS sound therapy (Spectral Activated Music of Natural Optimal Structure). The ear can only detect frequencies up to 15,000 Hz, but the brain can detect frequencies above that. Research has found that high frequency tones above 15,000 Hz are more therapeutic. Great results have been seen in people with a wide diversity of problems including speech and voice problems, perceptual disturbances, anxiety problems, deafness, autism, Down Syndrome, learning difficulties, and more (Forrest Lien).

One Family's Story

On a personal note, Kathleen D. Moore offers an account of her family's adoption of a three and a half year-old Bulgarian boy and her experience working with her son. She sought therapy for him and worked with Deborah Gray for two years, and talks about the techniques Deborah taught her and her husband to encourage bonding and trust in day to day family life.

Kathleen and her husband allowed Gregory to interact only with them at the beginning so that he would learn to rely on them to fill his needs. She expresses that this was difficult, as it required constant vigilance. They limited his interaction at the dinner table, making themselves his only source of food, drink and comfort, touching him while eating to bridge his needs to their nurturing. When he was hurt they comforted him and encouraged him to cry—however, he did not allow himself to cry for months after they started working on attachment. They encouraged eye contact and touching. They rocked him to sleep for the first six months, allowing for hours of touching, singing and gazing, stroking his face and arms as they sang or gazed. They bottle fed him for a few minutes every day, emphasizing eye contact, and massaged him. A portrait of the family was hung which included him. Gregory did not always respond well and made every effort to sabotage them. It took immense effort and will, but the result is that although he still has problems with trust, safety, control and authority, he loves his family.

Care for the Caregiver

Therapy for the parents can be just as essential as it is for the child. "It is important that [parents] get in touch with the sadness and disappointment they are experiencing over losing the dream they had of having a 'normal, loving child.' For parents for whom the appropriate therapy is not available for their child," Moore stresses, "The goal with the difficult child is to provide consistency and predictability. What is most predictable is that the child can trust the parent; they can count on the parent to come through with the positives for good behaviour just as much as they can count on the negative consequences for unacceptable behaviour."

Moore suggests humour for parents who need an outlet, a release for their deeper, darker feelings. "The mother has a higher risk level for losing her feelings of confidence and self-worth, especially with respect to her parenting skills and the frustration, hurt, confusion the mother feels are frequently expressed in the form of constant complaints, anger or even blame. A technique called checking it out can be used between the parents, where, for example, the mother may ask her husband if he feels she has done as poorly in her parenting as she feels she has.... His understanding and empathy are extremely important, acknowledging the pain, frustration and anger she has in dealing with such a difficult child." (Odenthal, S.G.)

Further Reading

There is much literature available through the SNAP library regarding attachment disorder and its treatment. The Internet is also a good source, and the Attachment Center at Evergreen has a web site at: www.attachmentcenter.org.

This article originally appeared in the SNAP newsletter, Vol. 16 #2, summer 2000. © 2000 Society of Special Needs Adoptive Parents.

Hope for the Future:

An Adoptive Parent's Perspective

by Tanya Helton-Roberts

Once upon a time there was a family. Drinking and violence were common, even though the 1950s society around them was relatively restrained. Social workers tried to help, providing job training and encouraging them to take better care of their children. Yet their children grew up in a violent uncertain world. They did not know how to have safe relationships. They married.

One of these families had a daughter, Karen. At a young age she learned how to take care of herself, stealing food when she was hungry, ducking when blows were directed at her. When she was one a brother was born, Billy. The two of them quickly learned to please the adults around them. Strangers were often around, a lot of the time their mom and dad were in the basement having a party. Sometimes there was no food, and most of the time they wore their diapers for extended periods of time. Sometimes social workers came over. Their mom claimed to be separated from their dad so she could get more welfare money, but he was there off and on. One time their aunt was so upset with what she saw that she called the social workers. When the social workers were around the kids were fed and cleaned up. But that didn't last long. Their mom had another baby, but this was a big handful for anybody. And it was too much for their mom especially. She put the baby in the crib and locked the doors of Karen and Billy's bedrooms. They were used to the hooks that kept their doors closed for hours at a time. But this was a hot day and their sour bottles didn't last long. They lay there waiting for someone to remember they were there. Their mom was having a party in the basement; it was cool down there. She figured that having a few friends over and having a good party would help her forget all the frustration she felt dealing with those kids. It was getting cool down there so she turned up the heat. Upstairs the children sat in locked rooms. The temperature soared well above 30 degrees. Finally someone came.

The nurses told them they didn't have to go back to their mom. And their baby brother hadn't made it. The malnutrition and dehydration was too much for him, but the other kids managed to survive – just barely. The doctor said that if it had been a few minutes longer Billy would have died too. They went and stayed at a foster home. They had a swimming pool and they let them do fun stuff. One day they heard that their mom had just had another baby but he was staying at a different foster home so they hardly saw him.

Once upon a time there was another family. There was a mom and a dad and a little girl. They wanted more children in their family. The adoption worker called one day to tell them that they would get a girl, a boy, and a baby. Just what they wanted.

But the new little girl would go with strangers, especially men. Her new mom was really embarrassed when she put her hands all over them. And she didn't know what to do when she found bags of urine hidden in the closet.

There were lots of other weird things that happened. You probably wouldn't believe the adoptive family if they told you. But nobody ever knew how to help them. That little girl grew up and ran away from home. She lived with a lot of guys. She decided that she would get more money from welfare if she had a baby. And she did. They bought her a new crib and food, and lots of new clothes. She got a lot of attention too. She had the baby, but people kept paying attention to the baby. She only got attention if she held the baby so she did, once in awhile. But she didn't want a girl. She had wanted a boy to replace her brother that had died. So she called the baby, 'The Kid'. She didn't feed her all the time, and once in awhile she hit her. This baby always needed her and didn't help her the way she wanted. When the baby was one she got a new boyfriend. He liked the baby and took care of her so her mom didn't have to. And she didn't ask what happened in the bathroom when The Kid cried. One day the police and a social worker came. Somebody had reported seeing bruises on The Kid. Her mom screamed and made it clear to the police officer that he was not going to take her kid without a fight. He took the baby and left. The Kid didn't know what to expect.

The Kid was now one and a half. She was in a foster home for several months before a judge told her mom and stepdad she could go home. Back to the touching, and the bruises. They had a baby a couple weeks later. He was a boy and that was better than being a girl. He got a lot of attention because his mom liked boys.

But a few months later it was too much for their mom. She did not want to keep the brats, especially since her boyfriend had left. It was late when she phoned her adoptive parents and said, ' Come and get the kids or I am going to kill them'.

This is just one of the many attachment stories out there. It is a story of real attachment and unattachment. The little girl who grew up to be an abusive mom was my adopted sister. And her little girl, The Kid, is now my adopted daughter. My daughter had severe attachment symptoms when I adopted her at age two. At age three she received attachment-based treatment in the United States and now functions as an active nine-year-old (although we still have some interesting moments).

Attachment is becoming a buzzword in parenting circles and certainly in adoptive circles. Recent television documentaries on attachment disorder, including 20/20, as well as in storylines in dramas such as episodes on Chicago Hope and CSI, have raised public awareness of what happens when children do not attach. Yet professionals remain largely uninformed and lack practical knowledge of the symptoms of attachment. This means that parents are often responsible for doing the groundwork, buying hundreds of dollars worth of books and resources, long-distance calls, and hours of heartache seeking the magical answer on how to get their children appropriately diagnosed. Unfortunately, after this long struggle, those parents who do find someone capable of recognising the problem are told that that there is little or no treatment available in Canada and no hope for their child. At this point parents often become involved with social services and psychologists who have little or no understanding of the issue, and experience the secondary trauma of being judged for their parenting skills rather than being offered appropriate support and resources. Parents from across Canada are trying to convince officials that they are not the crazy ones and trying to find help before their child is too old.

We need help. We need treatment programs across the country and this has to happen soon. Attachment must become the foundational element in all adoption and foster placements and the parents must receive appropriate support. Children who do not receive assistance grow up to become dysfunctional themselves.

I am a life coach for parents of children with severe behaviour problems. Most of their children have attachment difficulties. I hope that one day we will have full-service treatment facilities that provide support, practical life strategies, empathy, and training. It is the only hope if we are to reach the dysfunctional children who will one day be parents.

identity

WHEN I WAS GROWING UP,
PEOPLE WOULD ASK ME WHERE
MY REAL PARENTS WERE. I TOLD
THEM 'AT HOME.'
– Adopted person

What Children Understand About Adoption at Different Ages

by Lois Melina

Children cannot understand adoption until they can understand reproduction, usually around the age of 6. Nevertheless, many experts believe children should hear about their adoption before this age.

Early discussions ensure that children will hear about their adoptions from their parents in a loving, positive way, rather than as a taunt from a neighbor's child. Furthermore, children often sense that there is a secret about them and conclude it must be bad if no one will talk about it. Parents can introduce the subject by paying attention to natural, appropriate opportunities to do so.

Natural, appropriate opportunities are those times when adoption is relevant. For example, introducing a child as my adopted daughter Bianca is no more appropriate than introducing a child as my prematurely born daughter Bianca. However, it is appropriate for parents to say, as they tuck a child in bed at night and get a warm feeling about having that child, "I'm so glad we adopted you."

Preschoolers

When a child is old enough to listen to brief, simple stories, one of those stories can be the story of her adoption. The story will probably sound something like this:

Mommy and Daddy wanted a baby very much, but couldn't make one that would grow inside Mommy. You grew inside another woman. But she and your birth father couldn't take care of any baby born to them at that time in their lives, so you came to live with us. I'm sure they were sad, and you may have been sad, too. I was sad that you weren't born to us, but now we're happy that we're a family, and I think your birth parents are happy to know you're being taken care of.

Simple as it is, that narrative provides the framework for future discussions of adoption. As children get older, parents can add more details about their infertility, the birth mother and birth father, the process they went through to adopt, and why the birth parents were unable to care for any baby at that time.

Parents shouldn't be fooled into thinking their young child understands adoption because he is able to repeat the story. He is probably just parroting what he's been told. He must first understand time and space in new ways before he can truly understand how he joined his family. That ability begins around the age of four.

Around that age, children begin to understand that some things happened in the past even though they have no memory of them, and that some things will happen in the future. Similarly, they can understand that places exist outside of their immediate environment.

Out of this new cognitive ability comes an awareness that they were not always as they are now. They were once babies, and someday they might be mommies or daddies. Eventually this leads children to ask, "Did I grow inside you, Mommy?"

It's important for adoptive parents to realize that the child probably is not asking whether she was adopted, but whether she grew inside her mother, as she's been hearing that babies do. She naturally asks the only mother she knows—her adoptive mother.

Parents need to respond to the question the child is asking by reassuring the child that she did indeed grow inside a woman and that she was born the way all children are born. Then, parents can add that after the child was born, because her birth parents couldn't take care of any child born to them at that time, she came to live with her adoptive parents.

Middle childhood

Children tend to become more curious about adoption during the middle childhood years - approximately ages 7 to 11. During the information-gathering years of elementary school, children are interested in many details about themselves, such as whether their birth parents were married, whether they have any biologic brothers or sisters, how old their birth parents are and where they live.

This is also a time when they realize that most other children are living with at least one biologic relative, and they come to understand that the way they joined their families is somewhat unusual. It isn't uncommon for them to experience hurt, anger, or sadness at what may feel like abandonment or rejection to them. They may grieve for the loss of connections to their birth relatives - even though they are happy to be in their adoptive families. Because they don't fully understand why they couldn't remain with their birth parents, they may feel that their security in their adoptive family is shaky.

Not all this may be immediately apparent, however. Children in the middle childhood years may not initiate discussions about adoption with their parents. Their new problem-solving capabilities may lead them to erroneous conclusions about how and why they were placed for adoption, and they may not see any need to discuss them. They may find the topic too painful to bring up. And because around this time they develop the ability to think without using words, they may not even know that the sometimes confusing, sometimes uncomfortable feelings they occasionally have are related to being adopted.

For this reason, parents need to continue to bring up the topic whenever it seems appropriate. By being alert to cues that a child is dealing with an adoption issue, parents can bring the subject out into the open. For example, after strolling through the mall with their child, a parent who adopted a child locally might say, *Do you ever wonder if you're walking past birth relatives without even knowing it?* When a child shows a particular aptitude or ability, a parent could say, *I wonder if your birth father was a tall like you and a good basketball player—have you ever thought about that?*

This is a good time to take advantage of contact with the birth parents that may be possible directly or through the adoption facilitator. By contacting the birth parents, children can get information as well as an answer to the important question of why they were placed for adoption from the most credible source.

Parents shouldn't get caught up in always providing their child with the answers to her questions. There is value in discovering truth on one's own. By helping a child work through questions herself or allowing her to write to the birth parents directly, yet remaining available to correct misconceptions or get faulty reasoning back on track, parents can serve their child better than they could even by handing her a file folder thick with information about her origins.

Adolescence

During adolescence, children firm up their sense of personal identity and begin to assert their independence. Adolescents who are adopted are interested in information about who they are and how they are unique individuals. They reflect on their parents and siblings to determine how they are alike and different from them. They are interested in details about their birth families, including the physical appearance of their birth parents and their ethnic background.

Teenagers may not be sharing their questions about their origins with their parents, and may deny any interest in their birth parents if asked. Teenagers tend to guard their thoughts about themselves, especially from their parents.

Furthermore, adolescence is such a tumultuous time that many teenagers look for simple solutions to their problems. Some may think they would feel more content if they had information about their birth parents, but others may not realize they have concerns about adoption, thinking their life would be perfect if only they had a date for Saturday night, lost 10 pounds, or owned a car.

Parents may find it more effective to discuss adoption with their adolescents if they try to do so impersonally, discussing a hypothetical situation or a character in a movie or book.

They may also find their teenagers more willing to discuss adoption with other adopted teenagers, such as in a support group for adopted teens.

Children's interest in adoption ebbs and peaks within developmental stages. During the early part of a new developmental stage, as their mental ability changes to allow them to view adoption differently, they often have more concerns or questions about adoption.

As they progress through a developmental stage, their ability to understand new aspects of adoption improves, and their need to work through adoption issues may decline until they reach the next stage of development.

This article appears on Lois Melina's web site, www.raisingadoptedchildren.com. It is reprinted here with permission of the author.

Identity Issues for Adopted Teens
by Ellen Halliday

I am not adopted and had never done any reading on the matter until I started volunteering at SNAP. Having been a teenager, I can relate to the identity issues all teenagers face, but found it especially interesting to discover that adopted children often make up identities for themselves due to a lack of information about their birth parents. This is the issue that most impressed me in the reading I did. It does not mean there are not other issues adopted teens face—the SNAP library has lots of very good information on the subject for anyone who wishes to do further reading.

Special Teens, Special Challenges
For the most part, the lives of adopted children turn out very well. Like everyone else, they experience difficulties during adolescence, but of a different degree.

Adolescence stretches from about the age of 11 to around 18. Adolescence is typically about finding one's identity and separating from the family, physically and emotionally—figuring out who you are in relation to your family, your peers and society. Adolescents begin to think in abstract terms, to manipulate and explore ideas, and to understand and apply concepts without specific concrete examples. Teens can begin to imagine themselves being different people, and taking on different identities. Since identity is established partly by seeing how you are different from and the same as your family, adopted children face an unknown or partially unknown variable: their biological parents. When information is missing about the circumstances of their adoption, they may make up their own theories of what happened and who they are. They may ask: *Who were my birth parents? What were they like? Do I look like them? Will I be like them? Why did they put me up for adoption? Because I was bad?*

Piecing Together an Identity

Adopted adolescents without knowledge of their birth parents (or even with some knowledge) may begin to imagine themselves in ways for which they have no reference point. They may think that their parents were careless to have had a baby so young or that they were irresponsible, promiscuous, or bad. They can develop identities for themselves based on what they think or imagine their parents could have been like, and adopt behaviours they imagine their birth parents may have had. They may have a curiosity about their medical background, whether there may be inheritable diseases or alcoholism. They may wonder how tall they will grow, what they will look like when older, whether they will be full chested or flat chested or whether they will unwittingly marry their birth brother or sister.

This is why it is important to be able to answer as many questions as possible about their birth parents:

> ... the more facts they have about their birth parents the better, as, even if this information is disturbing, it enables them to focus on understanding and accepting the truth, rather than trying to understand a myriad of possible truths—some of which may be more disturbing than the actual truth. (Melina, 1991)

It is not necessary to sugar-coat the circumstances of their birth or to lie; but it is important not to paint the birth parents as "bad" or to disparage them. Create an environment where it is okay to talk about the birth parents. A teen not asking questions isn't a sign the teen has no questions, but rather, may not be comfortable asking them. Some children may not ask out of loyalty to adoptive parents or out of fear of hurting them. However, it is important to keep revisiting the subject at different stages of your child's development as the information is integrated in different ways as they grow older.

Youth with Disabilities

Adopted children with disabilities may think they were rejected and put up for adoption strictly because of their disability. Disabled adoptees mourn not only the loss of their birth parents but also the loss of the person they wish they were. The identity issues adolescents face are compounded for them, and they may need help expressing their feelings of sadness and anger, and dealing with possible poor self-esteem issues and negative behaviour. People tend to see disabled people as their disability and forget they have the same needs and feelings as everyone else. It is important for disabled teens to have disabled adults as role models so that they can see that a disabled person is capable of contributing to society (be it as a mother, a father, a welder, etc.) as well as to have contact with other children with disabilities.

Racial Issues

Being an adopted child whose race is different than that of their adoptive parents and siblings adds another layer of confusion to the formation of an identity as they must deal with establishing a cultural identity. At adolescence, cultural conflicts may intensify as cultural questions are related to identity concerns. Transracially adopted teens may step away from the culture of their adoptive parents and toward the culture of their birth parents. They may feel isolated or rejected because their racial features are continual reminders that they are "different." Some may reject the racial identity of their adoptive parents and become obsessed with their own racial identity. There is a chance they could be rejected by both those of the race of their birth parents as well as by the race of their adoptive parents. Parents can help by raising their children to have an appreciation for their own culture and for racial diversity, and set an example by having friends of other races.

Grief and Loss

At adolescence, feelings of loss or grief over being adopted may come up or resurface as each new level of cognition brings a new connotation to the loss with which the adoptee must deal. The loss adopted children face is "... not only loss of birth family, but also loss of the person he or she would have been had he remained with his birth family" (Van Gulden & Bartels-Rab, 1993).

They may wish to make an attempt to find out more about their birth parents. It is important for teens to be able to explore and discuss their feelings about adoption. If teens feel the information they have about themselves and their birth parents is incomplete, it is important to be supportive of their attempts to obtain whatever information might be available from the agency.

All young people, adopted or not, go through a difficult time in their teens. For the majority of adopted children, adoption turns out to be very positive thing—it's just a matter of weathering the extra turbulence of those teen years.

Works Cited

Lois Melina. "Talking With Children About Adoption." *Ours* 1991 May/June, p. 13

Holly Van Gulden and Lisa Bartels-Rab. *Real Parents, Real Children.* (New York: The Crossroads Publishing Company, 1993)

This article originally appeared in the SNAP newsletter, Vol. 15 #3, Fall 1999. © 1999 Society of Special Needs Adoptive Parents

Speaking Positively:
Using Respectful Adoption Language
by Patricia Irwin Johnston

Respectful Adoption Language (RAL) is vocabulary relating to adoption which has been chosen to reflect maximum respect, dignity, responsibility and objectivity about the decisions made by birthparents and adoptive parents in discussing the family planning decisions they have made for children who have been adopted. First introduced by Minneapolis social worker Marietta Spencer as positive adoption language or constructive adoption language and evolving over the past 20 years, the use of RAL helps to eliminate the emotional overcharging which for many years has served to perpetuate a societally-held myth that adoption is a second-best and lesser-than alternative for all involved—that in being part of an adoption one has somehow missed out on a "real" family experience. The use of this vocabulary acknowledges those involved in adoption as thoughtful and responsible people, reassigns them authority and responsibility for their actions, and, by eliminating the emotionally-charged words which sometimes lead to a subconscious feeling of competition or conflict, helps to promote understanding among members of the adoption circle.

RAL begins with the concept of family. Historically people have been considered to be members of the same family when one or more of several conditions are met: they are linked by blood (father and son), they are linked by law (husband and wife), they are linked by social custom (woman and her husband's sister), they are linked by love. We don't blink at the concept of two non-genetically-related people being members of the same family if one or more of the other criteria are met...except in adoption.

Though in adoption parent and child are linked by love and by law, the fact that they are not connected by blood has often meant that some people are unwilling to acknowledge their relationship as genuine and permanent. Thus they use qualifiers ("This is Bill's adopted son") in situations where they would not dream of doing so in a non-adoptive family ("This is Bill's birth-control-failure son" or "This is Mary's caesarean-section daughter.") They tend not to assign a full and permanent relationship to persons related through adoption ("Do you have any children of your own? "or "Have you ever met your real mother?" or "Are they natural brothers and sisters?") They assume that adoptive relationships are tentative ("Will the agency take him back now that you know he's handicapped?" or "What if his real parents want him back?")

As the concept of family changes, it is important that we consistently acknowledge that any two people who choose to spend their lives committed to one another are indeed a family. A couple who has chosen a childfree lifestyle and a single parent with children are just as much families as is a married couple who has given birth to six children.

The reality is that adoption is a method of joining a family, just as is birth. It is a method of family planning, as are birth control pills or abortion. Though the impact of adoption must be acknowledged consistently in helping a person who has been adopted or one who has made an adoption to assimilate this issue positively, adoption should not be described as a "condition." In most articles or situations not centering on adoption (for example, during an introduction, in a news or feature story or an obituary about a business person or a celebrity) it is inappropriate to refer to the adoption at all. (An exception may be in an arrival announcement.) When it is appropriate to refer to the fact of adoption, it is correct to say "Kathy was adopted," (referring to the way in which she arrived in her family.) Phrasing it in the present tense—"Kathy is adopted"—implies that adoption is a disability with which to cope.

Those who conceive and give birth to a child are his *birthparents*: his *birthmother* and *birthfather*. All of us have birthparents, however not all of us live in the custody of our birthparents. Those who raise and nurture a child are his parents: his mother, father, mommy, daddy, etc.

In describing family relationships involving adoption it is best to AVOID such terms as *real parent, real mother, real father, real family*—terms which imply that adoptive relationships are artificial and tentative—as well as terms such as *natural parent* and *natural child*—terms which imply that in not being genetically linked we are less than whole or that our relationships are less important than are relationships by birth. Indeed in adoption children will always have TWO "real" families: one by birth and one by adoption. Similarly, when conscientiously using RAL, one would never refer to a child as *one of your own,* which intimates that genetic relationship is stronger and more enduring and adoptive relationships tentative and temporary.

In describing the decision-making process birthparents go through in considering adoption as an option for an untimely pregnancy, it is preferred to use terms which acknowledge them to be responsible and in control of their own decisions.

In the past, it is true, birthparents often had little choice about the outcome of an out-of-wedlock pregnancy. In earlier times they did indeed surrender, relinquish, give up and even sometimes abandon their children. These emotion-laden terms, conjuring up images of babies torn from the arms of unwilling parents, are no longer valid except in those unusual cases in which a birthparent's rights are involuntarily terminated by court action after abuse or neglect.

In an age of increasing acceptance of out-of-wedlock pregnancy and single parenthood, today's birthparents are generally well counseled and well informed about their options, and using Respectful Adoption Language acknowledges this reality. Increasingly, as agencies take on the role of facilitator and mediator rather than lifter-of-burdens and grantor-of-children, the phrase *place for adoption* is also being questioned. The preferred RAL terms to describe birthparents' adoption decisions are *make an adoption plan, plan an adoption* or *choose adoption* ("Linda chose adoption for her baby.") Well counseled birthparents who do not decide on adoption do not *keep* their babies (children are not possessions) but instead they *choose to parent* them ("After considering her options, Paula decided to parent her child herself.")

The process by which families prepare themselves to become parents is often referred to as a *homestudy.* This term carries with it an old view of the process as a weeding out or judgment. Today, more and more agencies are coming to view their role as less God-like and more facilitative. The preferred positive term, then, is *parent preparation,* a process whereby agency and prospective adopters come to know one another and work toward expanding a family.

As both sets of parents consider the ways in which they may plan an adoption their choices include retaining their privacy in a *traditional* or *confidential* (not closed) adoption or they may opt to have varying degrees of ongoing contact between birthparents and adopters in a process commonly known as open adoption. Some adopters parent children born outside the U.S. in a style of adoption respectfully referred to as *international adoption.* The older term *foreign* has negative connotations in other uses and so is now discouraged. Similarly, adopters who choose to parent one or more older children, sibling groups, or children facing physical or emotional or mental challenges are said to be parenting *children with special needs* or *waiting children,* terms seen as potentially less damaging to the self esteem of these children than the older term *hard-to-place.*

While adoption is not a handicap, it is a life-long process. Frequently news stories refer to *reunions* between people who are related genetically but have not been raised in the same family. In most such instances these encounters do not carry with them the full spectrum of understanding that the usual use of the term reunion implies. While children adopted at an older age may indeed experience a reunion, most adoptees join their families as infants and as such they have no common store of memories or experience such as are traditionally shared in a reunion. The more objective descriptor for a meeting between a child and the birthparents who planned his adoption (a term which neither boosts unrealistic expectations for the event nor implies a competition for loyalties between birthparents and adoptive parents) is *meeting.*

This short poem by Rita Laws first seen in *OURS: the Magazine of Adoptive Families* (now *Adoptive Families*) attempts to point out humorously the impact of negative language in adoption...

Four Adoption Terms Defined
Natural child: any child who is not artificial.
Real parent: any parent who is not imaginary.
Your own child: any child who is not someone else's child.
Adopted child: a natural child, with a real parent, who is all my own.

Positive Adoption Language, however, is very serious business. Just as in advertising we choose our words carefully to portray a positive image of the product we endorse (selling Mustangs rather than Tortoises, New Yorkers rather than Podunkers), and in politics we take great care to use terminology seen positively by the class or group of people it describes, those of us who feel that adoption is a beautiful and healthy way to form a family and a responsible and respectable alternative to other forms of family planning, ask that you consider the language you use very carefully when speaking about those of us who are touched by adoption!

This material has been adapted and excerpted from *Adopting After Infertility* by infertility and adoption educator Patricia Irwin Johnston (copyright 1992). This version is reprinted with permission of the author.

open adoption

I THINK WITH THE INCREASE IN ...OPEN ADOPTIONS THERE'S A RECOGNITION THAT, ALTHOUGH MAYBE TRADITIONALLY WE WOULD SEE THOSE TWO PARTIES AS BEING RIVALS OR SOMEHOW BEING AT ODDS WITH ONE ANOTHER OR COMPETING, IN FACT, IF THEY'RE THINKING OF THE CHILD AND THE CHILD'S WELFARE, THEN IT'S DIFFERENT.

– Pat Fenton, Adoption Council of Ontario

The Trend Toward Open Adoption in Infant & "Waiting Child" Placements

by Bruce Regier

Some degree of openness is commonly practiced in nearly all infant adoption placements in BC and, more and more, it is becoming a trend in the adoption of BC's "Waiting Children." Still, many prospective adoptive parents are unfamiliar with the concept of open adoption. In the past, it was believed that secrecy was necessary to protect the parties involved, particularly in light of attitudes toward "illegitimate" children; but now attitudes have changed. Many experienced with adoption practices draw a distinction between openness in adoption (or semi-open adoption) and true (fully) open adoption. Openness includes a broad range of communication between adoptive parents, adoptees, and birth parents. It can include exchanging letters and pictures; meeting but only exchanging first names; communicating through an intermediary such as an adoption agency; or any number of variations short of a fully open arrangement.

Meeting Real People

To many prospective adoptive parents, limited openness makes sense, but the notion of open adoption often seems, well, just too far out. Before adopting our son, my wife and I felt that way ourselves. But, like many other adoptive parents who have experienced open adoption, our fears disappeared once we met our son's birth mother and had a chance to get to know her and our son's birth grandmother. Meeting real people dispelled our fears and we found that our son's birth mother and birth grandmother were very respectful toward us. The birth mother recognized us as parents from the beginning because that is what she wanted us to be.

In the long run, we believe that this relationship is best for our son. He has unlimited access to information about his birth family's past so that any natural curiosity about his heritage can be addressed. There is no need for him to become obsessed with unanswered questions. If he ever experiences a health crisis, we have not only written medical history, but access to detailed information from his birth parents. He has permission to care about his birth parents and develop a relationship with them, if he wishes, without feeling guilty or worrying that his adoptive parents will not understand. He will also have a strong sense of belonging within our family, since he will know that his birth mother selected us to raise him and placed him personally in my wife's arms. Because it is better for him, it is better for us as adoptive parents. We do not have to deal with unknown birth parents and develop false characteristics about them in our minds or the mind of our child over time. It is also better for our son's birth mother. I am sure she has and will continue to grieve over the loss of her son, but, hopefully, she will be better able to deal with those feelings in the context of open adoption. She has had the opportunity to make choices, plan for her child's future, and choose the parents who would raise him. Over time, she will know that her son is thriving in a good home.

Does Openness Make Sense with Foster Children?
Of course, all of this is said in the context of infant adoption placement; many adopted children come from the foster care system. While many believe that placements should always be closed in these cases, more and more of those in the adoption community are considering the idea of open adoption in the placement of "waiting children" from foster care. Does openness make sense in these situations? Well, sometimes it does, but often it does not. If it is a viable option, it is often necessary to have very clear boundaries or a limited degree of openness rather than an arrangement that is as open as those we often see with infant placement.

Children end up in foster care because they have been removed from their birth families due to abuse and neglect. Typically, their birth parents have challenges that might include mental illness, substance abuse issues, violent behavior or felonious behavior. As a result, if you are considering any degree of openness it is essential to recognize behaviors that are malicious and intentionally harmful from those that are maladaptive in some way. If a birth family member has perpetrated malicious abuse, the child should not be subject to contact until he is mature enough to choose for himself.

If the birth parent or other birth family member is not a threat to the child or members of the adoptive family, openness may be very beneficial for the same reasons that it is beneficial in infant placements. It is important that we help our adopted children to understand and come to terms with the reasons they are not being raised within their birth families; openness can help us in this regard. However, when you are dealing with dysfunctional birth parents it is important to set boundaries and manage the risks.

It is up to the adoptive parents to maintain control of the situation and this can be a heavy burden. It is beyond the scope of what I can cover here to address at any length all of the potential dynamics that might be encountered; however, there is one general rule I can suggest. I would strongly recommend starting out with a conservative level of openness and setting a few clear boundaries in a written agreement. I would also recommend seeking a counsellor or mediator who understands adoption and openness issues to help you wade through the challenges.

When we adopt a child we cannot just forget our children's history and we cannot forget the people who have been important in their lives. This fact is even more significant in the adoption of older children and, in most cases, some degree of openness is definitely worth considering.

A portion of this article was first printed in *Focus on Adoption* magazine Vol. 6, No. 1, Feb/March,1998. It is reprinted here with permission of the author.

Adoption & Special Needs

by Lissa Cowan

Many of our readers understand the concept of open adoption yet there may be aspects that remain unclear. Just how "open" is open adoption? How can it benefit a child who has special needs? Are there limits as to when the birthparents can see the child? Can open adoption sometimes backfire for an adoptee hoping for answers from birthparents? Won't open adoption confuse the child even more?

Older adoptees who have special needs often have attachments to their birthparents that those who are adopted as infants don't. A child who has special needs may have been the victim of traumatic events involving abuse or neglect. Openness may allow for a child's healthy movement through the grief process as a result of hearing the adoption story from the birth family. This way the child need not act out or fantasize negatively about the parents. Also, having contact with siblings and former foster parents is important for children who have special needs. Deborah N. Silverstein and Sharon Kaplan Roszia write in their article titled "Openness: A Critical Component of Special Needs Adoption" that when a child knows both the birth and adoptive parents he or she is able to integrate a whole identity and create a multifaceted sense of self. This becomes especially important when children are adopted transracially or transculturally. Having exposure to their racial and cultural heritage offers knowledge about themselves and their families that the adoptive parents might not be able to provide. Adoption expert David Kirk (1985) also speaks of the advantage to adoptive parents because, in coming to know the birth family, they are better able to understand and accept their children's histories and the differences between themselves and their children.

A History

Although open adoption seems to be a relatively recent idea, in reality it has existed for centuries. In the past, grandparents, uncles and aunts often raised children not born to them but whose parents they knew.

The open adoption movement began in the 1960s in an attempt to eradicate the code of secrecy around adoption. Prior to this time most birthmothers had no control or knowledge over who would adopt their children. The birthmother might have seen her child once or twice after delivery, or not at all. Years later, when asking the adoption agency questions about her child and the adoptive parents, she might have been viewed as an intrusive stranger wishing to disrupt the life of a newly formed family.

Likewise, adoptees were often made to feel that desiring knowledge about their biological and cultural heritage was antithetical to their personal growth. Adoptees had many questions about their pasts, but no answers were provided by the "system". Part of this desire for secrecy was linked to the fact that governments and adoption agencies believed they were protecting the children. Many felt that contact by birthparents might impede the attachment process with the adoptive parents. For the agencies, the process was over after placement; thus, end of story. Of course that wasn't the case for many adoptees and their biological parents.

Within the past 20 years we've gone from believing that secrecy protects the adopted child to believing it could actually harm him or her. By the late 1980's, several agencies increased communication and contact between biological families and adoptive families (Bradbury and Marsh 1988). Today, though still controversial, open adoption is quickly becoming standard practice. Arguments in favour of open adoption relate to assuring the biological parents that a good home was chosen for their children and to giving parents an opportunity to know their child in the future. In open adoptions, biological parents appear to be less often hit with feelings of grief and loss. A recent study in the United States involving one-hundred-and-six teens said that the decision about whether or not to have their babies adopted hinged on never being able to see the child again and not knowing whether the child was adopted into a safe and loving home. Other arguments for open adoption relate to lessening emotional problems experienced by adoptees. It has been documented that these problems, which are linked to a child's sense of identity, continue unresolved as he or she grows up. Adding to this are feelings of rejection by their birthparents, and having a lack of heritage.

Disquieting Loneliness

In his book Roots, Arthur Haley talks about "disquieting loneliness". This expression accurately describes the feeling of many adoptees, haunted by their pasts that remain a mystery. Elizabeth Lewis Rompf writes, "knowledge of one's biological history constitutes an innate human need" (Open Adoption: What Does the 'Average Person' Think?) Yet how to fulfill this human need without upsetting the delicate balance that is the adoptive family?

Degrees of Openness

It seems that many members of the adoption triad agree that a certain amount of openness is necessary, however, the question is what degree of openness is appropriate? Degrees of openness generally depend on the comfort levels of both the biological parents and adoptive parents. It might help to look at open adoption less as a label and more as a connection between people, or, "more a relationship than an institution or a process" (Melina & Roszia 1993: xviii). It's a fact that every adoption involves a unique group of adoptive parents, birthparents and children bringing their own unique personalities and histories (*Washington Parent Magazine*, "Adoption in the Future: A Trend Toward Openness,"Ann Humphrey). Because of this uniqueness, and due to the fact that adoptive parents, adoptees and biological parents are all vulnerable as a result of social and personal conditions that make adoption necessary, degrees of openness must be arrived at one step at a time. What seems to be important is giving both biological and adoptive parents full range of choices as to the amount of openness. Confidentiality and postplacement contact problems could occur when agreements between parties are not clear, or, when one person oversteps the boundaries.

This article originally appeared in the SNAP newsmagazine, Vol. 17 #5, September/October 2001. © 2001 Society of Special Needs Adoptive Parents

Open Adoption, Straight Up:
What Happens in Open Adoption?
by Jennifer Lee

For many of us, the term *open adoption* is a complex one; it is vague, confusing and sometimes frightening. Openness is a relatively new concept in adoption and one that has only gained in popularity in recent years. How does open adoption work and what do British Columbians need to know before they consider openness as an option for their pending or completed adoption?

What Open Adoption Means

Open adoption means, simply, that both birth and adoptive families exchange some communication and/or information prior, during or after the adoption process. The simplicity is disarming, however, for openness is not always simple.

Openness can mean the exchange of non-identifying information like medical and ethnic history with no contact at all or it can mean full disclosure so that the adopted child will have a personal relationship with his/her birth family. And, of course, there are multiple possibilities for openness anywhere in between.

Open adoption can also mean that the birth parents have chosen the adoptive parents personally, either through letters and pictures or through a face-to-face meeting. This can be done through an adoption agency or through the BC Ministry of Children and Family Development. As well, the birth parents may wish to place the child with a family they know through something called *direct placement*, another form of open adoption. However, the adoptive family is still subject to a home study conducted by the Ministry.

Openness Agreements

Adoptive parents and birth families who wish to have an open relationship can create an openness agreement. The Ministry of Children and Family Development recommends that the families contact a facilitator (usually an adoption agency or ministry adoption representative) for this process.

The openness agreement lays out exactly what is expected of each party. However, it is important to note that these agreements can change and are not enforceable by law. The relationship between the adoptive and birth families may change as the families grow. As well, each party's involvement is voluntary and any of the participants can withdraw from the agreement at any time. Non-compliance with the agreement is not grounds for the termination of the adoption.

Families who have been involved with a closed adoption but who now wish to have contact can register with the Post-Adoption Openness Registry. Because it is a passive registry, both adoptive and birth families must register before any contact can be made. Once that happens, the Registry asks the families to draw up an openness agreement with a facilitator. For an active search, families can contact the Adoption Reunion Registry, which conducts searches and provides counselling and support.

Because the Ministry does not monitor openness between adoptive and foster families, these relationships must be facilitated privately. Openness agreements can still be created and contact can still continue with foster families in the same way it does with birth families.

Although openness agreements in all situations are voluntary, it is still a necessary part of open adoption. It can help set boundaries and outline expectations.

Open adoption can be a complicated and emotional endeavour; however, if both the adoptive and birth families have agreed to openness in their relationship, they have done so in the best interest of the child and, ultimately, that is what matters.

Author's note: Much of the information in this article was taken from the Ministry of Children and Family Development website at www.mcf.gov.bc.ca/adoption.

This article originally appeared in the SNAP newsmagazine, Vol. 17 #5, September/October 2001. © 2001 Society of Special Needs Adoptive Parents

Openness:
Benefits & Risks
by Elizabeth Newman

A Brief History

While the practice of open adoption is a relatively new trend that has been emerging across Canada for the past twenty years, it has been practiced in most cultures outside of the western world for centuries. Research shows that in aboriginal communities, children are not "owned" solely by their parents but are the responsibility and delight of the entire community.

In Canada and the United States, the movement towards increased openness in adoption began as the adopted children of the previous closed system moved into adulthood. When these adults considered raising families of their own, identity issues pertaining to a lack of information about their biological heritage were raised. Several activist groups were formed and a passionate fight for the right to access birth records and other identifying personal information ensued. Birthparents also began to voice the pain and suffering they had experienced as a result of being cut off from information about the well being of their children. They also suffered from issues pertaining to complicated grief reactions due to the culturally induced shame and secrecy surrounding a crisis pregnancy.

It was becoming clear to many adoption workers that the traditional form of confidential adoption was not adequately meeting the needs of their clients. As society was moving toward greater honesty about many personal issues, experienced adoption workers explored the possibilities for more openness in adoption. In response, a significant body of research began to develop regarding the long-term outcomes in adoption adjustment. David Kirk, a professor from the University of Victoria, spearheaded some groundbreaking research acknowledging the differences between families who are formed through adoption and families who aren't. This "acknowledgement of difference" proved to facilitate empathic communication and enhance adjustment and satisfaction levels in adoptive children and their families.

The Benefits and Risks

The benefits of openness appear to outweigh the risks. Contact has allowed birth parents to have a sense of resolution regarding their decision to place their children. As birth parents have the opportunity to witness their children's healthy adjustment they have reported experiencing increased self-esteem because they believe they have made a good plan for their child. As contact with birth parents increases, adoptive parents have reported a decrease in fear regarding the birthmother wanting her child back. This has enhanced the attachment process between parent and child.

The risks involved in openness are similar to the risks involved in most relationships. These include the possibility of relationship breakdown, role confusion, boundary issues and disagreement regarding parenting style. Adoptive parents with more than one adopted child have expressed concern where one of their children may have contact with birth relatives and the other doesn't.

In successful openness arrangements, adoptive and birth parents seem to experience a 'good fit'. These people have reported having an attraction to one another during their early meetings. They have similar beliefs and values about life and relationships in general. They are very respectful of each other's boundaries and are careful about making assumptions regarding their relationship with one another. One adoptive parent's comment about her child's birthmother reflects this concept; "She does not push herself on our family. She is very respectful of our boundaries. Although we have let her know that we are happy to have her over however much she wants, she has created some boundaries for herself and I think that she needs to do that emotionally for her own sake." In successful open adoptions communication is open and fluid; if there is conflict or confusion it is discussed. These adoptive parents are also secure in their role as the child's primary caregivers and have worked through their grief associated with infertility and/or the loss of previous children.

The benefits of openness can be far reaching concerning the adopted child's identity development. Children who are in contact with their birth parents have increased access to information about their biological roots. This can profoundly affect the child's increased understanding of self. Access to such information can assist the child to more easily integrate the adoption experience over time, throughout each developmental stage. They are less haunted by a sense of abandonment because they are informed about their birth parents' reason for choosing adoption. They are also able to ask their birth parents questions, as they require increasing amounts of information. Adoptive parents are able to gain insight and understanding about their child's reactions and ways of being because they know the birth parent(s). One adoptive mother described her appreciation of this when she said, "Now when we have little problems with our child growing up and his personality, it's reassuring when I can call up and say, "What were you like when you were a kid? Did you do this?"" Many adoptive families who are in contact with their child's birth families have reported being thankful for having an extended support system and for knowing that their child is growing up surrounded by the love of two families.

For many families, open adoption has been a positive and growth promoting experience. Still, there are other situations in which openness has not been as successful. As our culture moves toward greater levels of openness in adoption, it is important to keep in mind that it may not be the right way for every one. Taking the time to consider individual values and beliefs, relationship skills and the 'good' or 'not so good fit' that adoptive parents and birth parents bring to an adoptive lifestyle is extremely important.

The author based this article, in part, on her master's thesis on open adoption. The article originally appeared in the September/October 2001 SNAP Newsmagazine, Vol. 17, No.5. © 2003 Society of Special Needs Adoptive Parents.

search
& reunion

IT HAS TAKEN SOME TIME, BUT
WE ARE NOW ABLE TO HAVE A
PLACE IN OUR HEARTS AND
MINDS FOR OUR DAUGHTER'S
BIRTH PARENTS. THEY ARE,
AFTER ALL, THE REASON WE
HAVE HER.

– Adoptive parent

Reunion:

What Adoptive Parrents Need to Know

by Harriet Fancott & Sara Graefe

In 1996, British Columbia's current *Adoption Act* was implemented and adoption records were opened. This raises the very real possibility that your child may want to search for and reunite with his/her birthparents. For adoptive parents, the prospect of reunion can raise painful emotions and conflicts, which can be further complicated by fears and misunderstanding around the process. We hope to clarify matters by discussing adoptive parents' concerns, fears, and feelings, and by examining possible outcomes of the reunion process.

Why Are Reunions Initiated?
Many birth parents never forget the child they placed for adoption. Many adopted people feel a deep desire to search for their birth parents to gain a clearer sense of themselves. Your child may be motivated to clarify his/her biological identity. This doesn't make your child any less connected to you.

Feelings and Fears
Reunion is a complex, emotionally charged process for all members of the adoption circle. As an adoptive parent, it is normal to experience a variety of intense feelings and fears. You may feel:
- worried that your child will be hurt or rejected by what s/he discovers
- threatened by the thought that the birth parent(s) may be more attractive or accomplished than you
- worried that you have failed as parents
- fearful that you will lose your child to the birth parent(s)
- concerned about the loss of future grandchildren
- anxious about the post-reunion relationship(s)
- grief over infertility-triggered loss
- betrayed by a government that promised adoption records would be sealed forever

It is important that you recognize and are able to express your feelings. Contrary to their fears, many adoptive parents find reunion to be a positive experience. Supporting your child's interest in reunion may ultimately strengthen your relationship with your child.

Talking about Reunion

Discussing adoption openly throughout childhood sets the stage to talk comfortably about reunion *(for more on talking to your child about adoption, please refer to the section of this book on Adoption and Identity Issues)*. Do not wait until your child starts to ask questions about reunion. Children may avoid telling you of their desire to know more about their birth parents because they don't want to hurt or disappoint you. Talking honestly about reunion helps relieve fears and anxieties for both you and your child, and allows you to support each other throughout the process.

Supporting Your Child

Your child needs you at this moment more than ever. Many adopted people feel abandoned by their birth parents. To experience rejection by you could have painful consequences.

Here are some tips on handling the subject of reunion:
- reassure your child that your love is unconditional and a reunion won't alter that fact
- do not make your child choose between your love and your child's desire to know his/her birth parents
- let your child dictate the pace and handle meetings
- support your child by keeping the lines of communication open

Outcomes

Each reunion is unique – it is important to consider and discuss a range of possible outcomes. Contact between a child and birth family can range from a one-time meeting, to an acquaintance-ship or friendship, to an ongoing familial connection. However, it is possible that your child could encounter a no-contact veto or outright rejection, the effects of which can be devastating. Prepare yourself and your child to deal with all of these possibilities.

Special Concerns for Parents of Children with Special Needs

As the adoptive parent of a child with special needs, you may be especially concerned about your child's ability to cope with the reunion process. You may fear for your child's health and safety due to special needs or, perhaps, the child's history with the birth family, especially if this involved abuse or neglect, or substance abuse.

These concerns are real and need to be acknowledged. However, under the current legislation, greater openness is now encouraged and more opportunities for reunion will occur. After your child reaches the age of 19, only your child and the birth parents have the authority to file a disclosure veto or a no-contact declaration. It is important that you begin to deal with the possibility of reunion, and take steps to support your child.

This article is adapted from the brochure, *Exploring Reunion: Fears, Feelings, Outcomes, Support,* developed by SNAP in partnership with AFA-BC and produced in cooperation with the BC Ministry for Children and Families, Adoption Division.
© 1996 Society of Special Needs Adoptive Parents

The Role of Adoptive Parents in Reunion
by Bob Creasy

Little has been written about the impact of adoption reunion on adoptive parents— the thoughts and feelings they experience can play a major role in the course of a reunion and can influence the quality of future relationship with their adult adoptee. Support from adoptive parents for search and reunion, or their opposition to reunion, certainly has an impact on the degree of comfort and openness an adoptee experiences in coping with reunion.

The parties involved in search and reunion, the so-called "adoption circle"— birth parents, adoptees, adoptive parents, all play a role in reunion. We need to be able to help them examine their feelings and attitudes without further entrenching positions that sometimes suddenly seem to be at war.

Often the first step in dealing with any kind of emotional pain is to correctly identify it. Identification can often reduce or remove the power of emotional pain to overwhelm us—as it can when we struggle to minimize it or to deny its existence.

Betrayal may be the first feeling adoptive parents experience when hearing about reunion. At the time of their application to adopt, they may have been assured that all adoption records were sealed forever and that they need not ever fear that a birth parent would find out who they were and come looking for the adoptee. This advice alone, can leave a sense of "hidden adversaries" with the adoptive parent, one which may or may not affect their relationship with their child during childhood, but one which might certainly colour attitudes toward the possibility of birth parent-adoptee contact.

Understanding why adoption laws have changed can often be helpful. Attending a support group or even talking to other adoptive parents can sometimes ease the feeling of betrayal, since doing these things can often "reset" the adoption in the context of changes and the present day, thereby giving a greater sense of participation and control to the adoptive parent who is struggling with feeling betrayed by changes to adoption legislation and practice.

Grief is another powerful feeling for adoptive parents in reunion. Grief may arise, in part, because reunion triggers issues of infertility or other birth preventive tragedies, as well as fear of loss of their adopted child. While infertility is not an issue in every adoptive situation, when it is, all of the pain associated with the inability to have a child can reappear when the child one has worked so hard in raising, suffered so much in loving, seeks or is sought by, his or her "natural parent."

The power of this rekindled grief, and the difficulty some have with its resolution, often points to the need for attention to be focused upon it again. We may feel great disappointment upon discovering that the "solutions" we applied to feelings in the past are no longer sufficient to the present circumstances which have been changed by reunion. Close friends, family members, and/or counsellors are often called upon to help with the process of healing. They fulfill the same roles they would fill in our lives under the conditions of deep bereavement.

It is very important to know that, as human beings, our first inclination with this kind of feeling (grief) is to underestimate and undervalue its magnitude and importance in our lives. The truth of the matter seems to be that we must re-experience this grief, at times go through a process of "re-grieving", in order to finally finish with the unhappiness of the past. These grief issues are one of the primary reasons why counselling services are now offered by adoption reunion agencies.

Adoptive parents may also feel devalued by the search and reunion process. There is a strong tendency to view contact between their son or daughter and a birth parent as a signal to themselves that their "stewardship" is over and their love, guidance, limits, cautions, etc. are no longer needed. This perspective is particularly detrimental in that it is usually a product of many other discouraging thoughts and feelings, especially the sometimes lifelong fear that the adoptee will "someday return to or be taken back by birth parents" (*Birth Bond*, Gediman, J. and Brown, L., 1991, p. 228).

This perspective is also dangerous because it profoundly effects the self-esteem of the adoptive parent and may cause them to question their legitimacy as parents. Thinking of oneself as "no longer necessary" can be the worst point of view you can take with respect to the needs of your child at this stage in his or her life.

Research and biographical data overwhelmingly indicate that your children do not feel that way about you.

Similarly, and particularly in post-reunion, an adoptive parent may feel competitive with birth parents. Many adoptive parents describe thoughts like, "I'll show him/her so much love that his/her relationship with the birth parent will just wither and die." This competition extends all the way from conflicts of religious conviction down to who makes a better meatloaf. It may be helpful to remember that in these competitive states, usually everyone loses. Isolation, anger, and depression can result from engagement in any "unwinnable" war.

This brief informational package cannot deal at length with the multitude of feelings and fears adoptive parents must face when their children seek or make contact with a birth parent. Some of these feelings and/or fears include:

- conscious or subconscious anger at the adoptee for being interested in the birthmother at all;
- worry that they may have failed the child, otherwise, why would he or she have to search?
- worry that the adoptee might be rejected by the birthmother, or hurt by what they may learn;
- concern that the birth mother will be more attractive than they (she could be ten or fifteen years younger)
- anxiety as to whether the post-reunion relationship will be brief or prolonged;
- worry about losing the grandchildren they have now or the ones yet to come.

A positive step can often be taken by the adoptee through reassuring his or her adoptive parents about the strength of their attachment and love. This can considerably reduce the sense of risking loss of their adopted child.

It is helpful if the effect of reunion can be viewed as adding "another dimension"—perhaps that dimension is being able to recognize what post-reunion can accomplish for adoptees:

- a sense of being real, normal adults just like everyone else;
- strengthened self-esteem after adoptees learn the circumstances of their birth and find out that they weren't "dumped";
- an end to the paralysis generated by all of the unknowns in their lives;
- a letting go of "the adoption difference" and replacing it with an unleashed potential to move on.

Many adoptive parents nurture their own security by staying informed and involved in reunion and post-reunion through offering support and reassurance to their child—support and reassurance are appropriate and important parenting roles which can be offered without, at the same time, interfering in the course of an adoptee's developing relationship with a birth parent.

There is more that an adoptive parent can do to help themselves and their sons and daughters through this difficult time. We offer the following suggestions in the hopes that you, the adoptive parent, can come to see that in spite of the difficulty search and reunion has brought into your life, there are also potential rewards for you in this process.

We suggest that you:

- get a copy of *Birth Bond* and spend some quiet time reading it;
- investigate counselling, either through our agency or though the local phone book;
- talk about your feelings and what is upsetting you with a trusted someone;
- understand your own boundaries. These are your personal limits. They are not walls, just clear, definitive statements of your values, tolerances (both physical and emotional) and wishes. A counsellor should be able to help you define these—reunion will change them;
- question your negative judgements of yourself.

The last thing we wish to say here is, that though it may be difficult to accept right now "the effect of reunion on the relationship between adoptees and their adoptive parents is almost always either to improve it or to have no effect: only rarely does it become worse"(Ibid, p229). How the process is viewed also seems to be a deciding factor in how emotionally trying the experience will be. Adoptive parents who have viewed the process as challenging consistently report positive outcomes. Adoptive parents who see the reunion process as a burden to bear, often must bear the burden longer.

Reference: *Birth Bond,* Gediman, Judith S. and Brown Linda P. Far Hills, New Jersey: New Horizon Press, 1991.

This article is a 1995 edit of an earlier article used in-house at the BC Adoption Reunion Registry, Family Services of Greater Vancouver. It is used here with permission of Family Services of Greater Vancouver.

For the Love of My Child:
An Adoptive Parent's Perspective
by Ellen Glazer

How long do we take to heal from the adoption experience? What impact does this early experience have on our lives? I came face to face with these issues one more time when I woke up from a nightmare with a feeling of terror deeper than I had ever experienced before. I got up and sat in the living room trying to catch

When Elizabeth was young, closed adoption was comfortable. But my outlook changed the day my teenage daughter said, "I want to find them."

The words, spoken quietly, were firm. "I want to find them," she said.

"Who?" I asked, though I knew.

"My birthparents."

"When do you want to try and find them ?"

"Now," she said.

And so the journey began.

I have always felt that birthparents are, for the most part, good people who make careful, thoughtful decisions they will abide by. I see adoptees searching to find answers — not new parents. And I believe that adoptive parents feel more secure when their children have the option, whether or not they act on it, to meet their birthparents.

But I find that I have a complicated view of openness in adoption. Although birthparents often select and meet adoptive parents, boundaries still exist, even in so-called open adoptions. Most are really semi-open, meaning that people met, exchanged information, then went on with their lives without requesting or anticipating ongoing contact. I believe that some degree of openness is best, especially for the child whose basic rights are in many ways vanquished by closed adoption. Nonetheless, I confess that there were ways in which my own closed adoption felt comfortable, easy, and uncomplicated. During Elizabeth's early years, I enjoyed the fact that she was all ours. I felt immense gratitude toward Elizabeth's birthparents, but little inclination to share her with them.

But things changed. Once Elizabeth was old enough to ask basic questions— What is my birthmother's name? Where does she live?—closed adoption no longer simplified things. How do you explain to your child that you don't know her birthmother's name? And how do you help a teenager who doesn't want to leave home for college when you know that it is because she has been through so many losses?

The Search Begins

A series of events that had the potential to confirm or contradict all my beliefs about adoption were set in motion by my shy and quiet teenage daughter's simple request.

Our first stop was the office of our social worker, Lisa Bray-Sinclair. Elizabeth's dad Don (from whom I have been divorced for several years), and I accompanied her and voiced our cautious support of her quest. "We support her searching, as long as she is ready," I said to Lisa. "We feel that she needs to have counseling or read some books first. We want very much for it to be a good experience, but we know that it can be immensely difficult."

Lisa respected our concerns. She would indeed recommend counseling, possibly a support group, and certainly some background reading. She also was in favor of Elizabeth accompanying me to an American Adoption Congress conference in Washington D.C.

The conference was, as we'd anticipated, a deeply moving experience. The high point was a session conducted by an adoptive mother and her daughter, who spoke of the daughter's search and reunion. For Elizabeth, the conference seemed to fortify her feelings. For the first time in her life, she heard other adoptees talk about their searches. She was given insights into the experiences of birthparents, and their love, determination, and pain had all been confirmed for her. For me, the conference nurtured a hope that Elizabeth and I would have a stronger relationship became of her search.

Elizabeth went to see Lisa after we returned home. She explained that her first step would be to send Elizabeth's birthmother a letter stating that she had information of interest to her. If it did not bring a response, she would follow up with a registered letter that said more. If that didn't work, we'd then discuss our next step.

At the time, I was certain that Elizabeth's birthmother would call immediately upon receiving the letter. I imagined the warm, emotional reunion they would have. It never occurred to me that she would not respond. Not to the first letter; not to the second. Not to Elizabeth's sweet note that followed, explaining that she only wanted information and, perhaps, a chance to meet.

Weeks passed. One day the phone rang; it was Elizabeth's quiet voice on the other end.

"Could you call Lisa?" she asked. "Could you ask her if I can have her first name?"

"Your birthmother's first name?"

"Yes."

"Of course. I'll ask her."

It was Cora. The nameless person, now Cora. An unusual name. Something to hold onto.

How does one mother understand another's failure to respond to a shared—and beloved—child? I did not take Cora's silence as rejection. Rather, I think it simply hurt her too much to call. Unfortunately, her silence must have caused Elizabeth immense hurt. I say "must have" because my soft-spoken daughter's response was simply to forge on without complaint. If Cora wouldn't call, maybe her birthfather would.

Lucky to be right this time. Bob responded immediately. Yes, of course, he wanted to meet Elizabeth. He was happy to hear from her and to know that she was okay. Yes!

All that matters now is that Elizabeth's birthfather did respond and turned out to be a terrific person. Knowing that my daughter would finally see her own flesh and blood gave me immense pleasure. And long before we ever met, I was tickled to think how happy Bob must be to have been found.

Elizabeth set the pace for the reunion, eager to make it happen soon. Her first meeting with Bob occurred only a week or so after he responded to Lisa's letter. When Elizabeth originally decided to search, I thought that her timing could not have been worse. Not only was she a high school senior, but she was clearly having a hard time leaving for college. She made it clear that she was unwilling to go far from home for college. Searching at a time when she was so vulnerable seemed like a bad idea.

Elizabeth knew when the time was right and pushed forward. Because her search turned out as it did, we are able to celebrate its many positive effects. Elizabeth enjoys an active campus life; she connects to us in more loving and positive ways; and she is more enthusiastic about school than ever before.

I used to worry about what would happen after the first or second or third meetings. What sort of relationships would unfold? How can it all work out?

Recently I got a phone message from Bob. He called to ask my advice about a gift for Elizabeth. He said two things that touched me deeply. One was, "I wanted your advice because you know her so much better than I do," and the other was, "I haven't heard much from Elizabeth. I'd like to see her more."

Since Elizabeth, like Bob, has a sentimental streak, I suggested that he get her a picture frame or an album. Then I offered some words of reassurance: "The fact that you don't hear from her frequently is a good sign. She knows you are there. She feels comfortable. She knows you're not going anyplace, and neither is she."

When Elizabeth found Bob, we all became part of an extended family. He and his son, Ben, came to family weekend at her college. I am especially excited about her 20th birthday, which we will be able to share together.

The Challenges We Face

Although the anticipation of family occasions with Bob gives me pleasure, there are aspects of this reunion that are challenging. One has been Bob's wife's reaction. She knew that many years ago, Bob had placed a baby for adoption, but I'm sure she had assumed that this would remain in the past. When Elizabeth came back into Bob's life, it complicated things a bit. Yet Elizabeth has been invited to their home on a number of occasions, and feels welcome there.

Another person having somewhat of a hard time is Elizabeth's younger sister, Mollie. Because she had grown up knowing where she came from, I admit that her feelings about this did not concern me. Elizabeth was the one who had been dealt the tough hand. Why worry about Mollie?

But when Elizabeth found Bob, she also found Ben and Hannah, his children, whom she promptly referred to as "my brother and my sister." Having only one sibling, Mollie was unnerved when Elizabeth suddenly had three.

A Lifelong Process

I adore Bob and am thrilled that he is in our lives. But I still cannot imagine what it would have been like for all of us to know each other over the years. What if Elizabeth had seen him on occasion? How would she have felt when he got married? And how would her loving relationship with Mollie have been impacted by Ben and Hannah?

People who are considering adoption are often told that it is a lifelong process. Elizabeth's search has underscored this for me. It is 'a process filled with contradiction and ambiguity. Thanks to Elizabeth and Bob, it is filled, also, with discovery, celebration, and wonder.

7 WAYS TO HELP A QUESTIONING CHILD

1. Make sure your child is emotionally ready before initiating birthparent contact.
2. Allow your child to set the pace and timing of the search.
3. See that she receives counseling, takes part in an adoptee support group and reads books on the subject.
4. Share details of the process with your child.
5. If the birthparent does not respond, help your child try not to feel rejected.
6. If and when reunion occurs, do not expect too much from your child; don't pressure her to share every little detail.
7. Don't forget other family members

—Ellen Glazer

A Father-Daughter Reunion:
In the Words of Elizabeth Glazer & Bob Naranjo

LIZ: It's hard to imagine that last year I had no idea who Bob was. Now, two years after my first visit to the social worker who helped me search, Bob and his other children, Ben and Hannah, are members of my extended family.

BOB: I know Liz waited a long time to see me, but I realized that I have been waiting a lot longer. Over the, years I thought of her often—on her birthday; when a friend had a baby; while my wife and I tried for three years before having our son, Ben. Imagine my joy when I saw the words, *Your birth daughter wants to contact you.*

LIZ: When Bob and I first met, there was an instant connection. He walked into the room, and it was like seeing myself in the mirror—without hair. It was especially nice for me since my sister, Mollie, is my parents' birth child, and for years I've been the only one in the family who didn't really look like anyone else. Bob and I look a lot alike, and that feels awesome!

BOB: Liz and I have much in common. Oreo cookie and grasshopper pie are our favorite ice-cream flavors, and we both love apple pie, tolerate blueberry pie, and don't like pecan pie. Neither of us likes golf, smoking, or extreme heights. We both love Civil War history and soft-rock music, hate country music, and love to help others. But parts of our reunion are difficult and challenging. One is figuring out my place in Liz' life.

LIZ: Bob is in my family to stay. He will always be a special part of my life. For the first time, I feel complete; I'm the happiest I've ever been. I feel that I know who I am and where I came from.

These companion articles originally appeared in *Adoptive Families* magazine, July/August 2001, pp. 41-43. Reprinted with permission from *Adoptive Families* magazine. For more articles like this one, to subscribe or to sign up for the monthly e-newsletter, visit *Adoptive Families* online, www.AdoptiveFamilies.com.

A Dream:

An Adopted Person's Perspective

by Sharon Jinkerson

How long do we take to heal from the adoption experience? What impact does this early experience have on our lives? I came face to face with this issues one more time when I woke up from a nightmare with a feeling of terror deeper than I had ever experienced before. I got up and sat in the living room trying to catch on to thoughts and feelings that were dark and confusing. As soon as I realized that my family was safe I burst into tears and began to release some of my anguish.

This was the eve of my thirty-seventh birthday. I waited all day for *"the call"* and thank God my birth mother didn't disappoint me. She had remembered this occasion—it, after all these years, was still a special day for her. I was thrilled and even allowed myself to be vulnerable and feel the relief and excitement.

Why then, was I sitting there terrified a few hours later? I sat alone in the middle of the night and allowed myself to recall the frightening images of my dream. A man appeared at my front door and began a rather innocuous conversation; I was wondering what he was doing at my doorstep when suddenly the dream turned ugly. The man began to force his way into my house. The dream moved faster and faster as I realized he was there to take my son. I tried to protect my baby but other people who I now recognized as social workers appeared and the struggle to keep my child in my arms became more and more hopeless. In vain I yelled at my partner to call 911 but he was frozen with terror and couldn't dial. At the split second when my son was finally being wrenched from my arms, I woke up.

As you might have guessed, I am a reunited adoptee. My birth mother and I had a wonderful conversation earlier that evening but I wanted to get down to all the details concerning my actual apprehension and subsequent adoption. As I carried on a rather pleasing conversation, I silently pondered many questions. What does she remember? What were her feelings at the time of the apprehension? But I didn't ask; I couldn't. I was frustrated with myself after all the years of personal growth and healing: I was still the loyal adoptee unable to address my own needs. I continued to "parent please" and have a safe, almost boring conversation with my birth mom. I wanted to hear her tell her story. What was she feeling the moment she first realized we would never see each other again? Instead, I croaked out a few vague questions about the past, but I ached as I allowed myself to wonder if I was a lovable baby.

My desire to know the truth became the catalyst for this nightmare. I experienced a scene buried deep within my soul. Although the myths and facts surrounding my early childhood are scattered and few, in my subconscious mind lay the full impact of the last panic moments with my family of origin. No matter how much I decide to deal with the issues surrounding my adoption, there at the base of my soul lies a scar that impacts every turn of my life especially in my role as a mother.

I was six months old when my father had a nervous breakdown. Apparently, the scene was ugly when the authorities removed my dad. I do not know if it was the stigma attached to mental illness or the stigma attached to the fact that my mother is native, but shortly thereafter, social workers came to remove my four brothers and me from our mother.

So why the dream? This particular dream is a psychological drama that has been played out over and over again in First Nations communities. At the age of six my grandmother and mother were both taken away from their family of origin to be raised in residential schools. My grandmother told of the loneliness and longing to live with family and practice their Anishanabe culture. She kept alive memories of home by sharing with other children in the few moments of privacy they were allowed. My grandmother was haunted by the terror they felt leaving home to face life in an institution. In this institution, they learned one cardinal rule, that dominant society had all the power.

I have no conscious memories of those final moments with my family but if the dream symbolically represented my apprehension, it told me I was terrorized as a infant and that a piece of me was taken at that moment never to be given back. It also allowed me to see inside my mother and feel the gravity of the situation.

This terror was not a familiar feeling to me. Of course, I was raised with the myth that adoption is a normal process. Accepting this, I learned to block out most of my feelings that came up surrounding the issue of my adoption. The feeling I was always able to acknowledge was curiosity. Where did all the anguish go? Like many adoptees, I was forced to rely upon the goodwill and good memories of various family members. After interviewing everyone except my birth mother, I was able to put together a sketchy picture of my history.

Some of the facts were always to haunt me. My adoptive mother was honest and explained to me that my physical condition upon the apprehension was bad. She said that I was suffering from malnutrition and a rash that looked like impetigo. This always made me think I was not really loved by my birth mother. In the aftermath of my apprehension, the social workers accused my birth mother of neglect. I always wondered why my non-identifying information that I received from the Adoption Division when I began my search reported that my mother loved me. I never knew what to make of this apparent contradiction.

Sometimes knowledge concerning our past comes in strange forms. In November of 1991 I gave birth to my son Solomon. His skin was a mess. His little legs, arms and face were covered in a painful looking rash that weeped and bled. Our family doctor tried unsuccessfully to treat it and we were referred to a skin specialist. By this time my son's skin was a shocking mess. We were told then that it was a simple hereditary skin condition that amounted to extremely dry skin. The doctor asked my partner and I if either of us had this as infants. The implications of this skin disorder with respect to my past were enormous. I began to consider as well, the allegations of my malnutrition. Perhaps it was a lack of finances and support. My mother was suddenly left alone in a place thousands of miles away from her family and culture.

It is a gift to know my skin condition was hereditary, that after looking after my son with daily baths and creams he was still a mess. It also became clear to me that my mother was not given any benefit of the doubt. She was an Indian in the fifties who was loving but negligent in the eyes of those social workers. Was caring for me the only item on the agenda? Perhaps it was their moral and social arrogance that caused them to decide my family's fate. There is no question I had a stable life, raised with a loving family. I am sure those social workers and the government were patting themselves on the back for a job well done. They had rescued an Indian child from malnutrition and a skin rash. We needn't look only to First Nation's communities to find examples of social injustice; age, sex, class and other racial issues resulted in many adoptions.

Social justice issues aside, what of the emotional pain that adoptees face in the aftermath of their adoption? I have a very typical adoptee profile. I've had difficulty trusting and belonging in my adult life. The decision to have family was extremely difficult. I was 34 years old before my son was born. I had always loved children but felt I was far too independent to have a family. Maybe that is what my mind processed but after that dream, I believe I was protecting myself from triggering my early life experiences. Although my adoption story is relatively traumatic, I now wonder what the impact is for people with more conventional adoption stories. It's clear that this experience is shattering for adoptees like myself. I have spent many hours tuning into my emotions which I believe lead me to this dream. Ultimately, I feel it was a passage into the future, that I needed to experience this horror in a context where I was safe and in control. As I cried, I knew they were healing tears; I was transcending this original pain.

No matter the rationale, these haunting shadows that reach back to the genesis of my being have shaped my life. The central cedar pole of my being that reaches up to the sky is rooted in pain and loss. At the age of thirty-seven, I was cast back decades to re-experience the emotional terror. As I got up from the chair, in the lonely hours before dawn, I couldn't help but peek in and reassure myself. Feeling each breath rushing in and out of my chest, each beat of my heart, I reached down and softly touched the face of my sleeping son.

This article originally appeared in the SNAP newsletter, Vol. 16 #1, Spring 2000. © 2000 Society of Special Needs Adoptive Parents

For more of Sharon's adoption story, see "To Bring Back Yesterday: The Story of First Nations Adoptions" in the Cross-Cultural section, page 167.

Letter to an Adoptive Father:
An Adopted Person's Perspective

Dad,

A lot of people have asked me about my dad and mom and what I thought of being adopted. I have thought about this for quite a while.

Someone once asked *don't you go visit your dad anymore?* And I said no. Transportation is a problem. But I really don't know if I can handle it. First I was brought into this world. Then abused by whoever, and my biological father didn't care. He was drinking and smoking pot with my biological mother. What kind of dad does that?

I'm quite proud of who I am, thanks to you and Mom. You opened your heart, your house to me. Gave me rules, love, care. You taught me things. You worked for years to support me, gave me what I needed.

And quite a few times I let you down, couldn't make you proud. Disrespected you. Fought with you. It was my fault. Now at age twenty, living with my girl friend has helped me realize that I'm sorry for hurting you.

You taught me right from wrong. You taught me how to build things. Do chores. Now once again, even though you're not here, I'm learning from you. Thank you for all you have done for me. Turning me into the person I turned out to be. You taught me how to love and respect everyone, not to abuse women or anyone period. You taught me manners and etiquette. You showed me a religion I believe in, and I wish to become closer to God. I hope I can learn to follow Him.

I don't want to turn out to be like my biological father. If I ever decide to visit him, again, I want to see you, my real dad, after seeing my biological dad. I say real dad because you did everything for me, not him. You love and care for me.

You looked after me, not him. You're the one I always remember and love. You're my real dad. I love you. Thanks for everything.

From your youngest son

This anonymous letter written by an adopted person originally appeared in the SNAP newsletter, Vol. 13 #3, Fall 1997. © 1997 Society of Special Needs Adoptive Parents

siblings

IF YOU FOCUS ON THE NEEDS
AND NUMBERS, THE "JOB" OF
ADOPTING SIBLINGS CAN SEEM
HUGE! WHEN YOU REALIZE THAT
THESE ARE CHILDREN NEEDING
A FAMILY, THE CONTEXT IS
DIFFERENT.

– Mark and Rae Johnson

Adoption & Siblings
by Tanya Helton-Roberts

In recent years many resources have become available to help birth parents, adoptive parents, and adopted children deal with their adoption circle experiences. However, there remains very little information regarding the impact of adoption upon siblings. There is some information and research available about whether or not birth siblings should be adopted together but there is a noticeable void regarding the impact of adoption upon siblings already in the home prior to the adoption, particularly when the adopted child has special needs. These children often have the most to lose in the adoption experience as the new child becomes the focus of the family and often remain so due to their intensive behavioural, emotional, or physical needs. The long-term impact of adoption on siblings must be a consideration for all adoptive parents.

Many siblings of adoptive children with special needs take on the role of 'parental child,'[1] being overly responsible to try to help their overwhelmed parents and gain some sense of control in the midst of chaos. Sensing the new demands on their parents, birth children often minimize their own needs and wants in order to lessen the load. This tendency may be heightened when the special needs child displays manipulative tactics, and where there is more than one child.

Siblings who are adopted together often display a strong bond that connects them at a level far deeper than that of adoption. Birth siblings represent one of the most basic levels of attachment, a permanent bond because they share one or both parents. The saying 'blood is thicker than water' is often disliked by adoptive families because it seems to minimize the depth of their love. However, it is often true of birth siblings. They have a strong forever bond even if their relationship is pathological. Siblings going into adoptive homes have lost their parental attachment figures so their siblings remain their only constant attachment, while providing them with a sense of permanent identity. 'I am the oldest,' 'I am a brother,' etc. all serve to give them a sense of security and a place in the world. If birth siblings are separated during foster care or adoptive placements, they frequently experience additional trauma as they lose the security of these ongoing connections.[1] This should be seriously considered in all placement decisions. That said, there are times when siblings should be separated. If one or more of the children has a serious personality disorder, such as Attachment Disorder, placing all of the children together heightens the risk of a disrupted placement or victimization of the other children.[2] Such severe behaviour children place increased demands upon the parents for supervision and care. Siblings with shared life experiences may display overlapping symptoms and placing them together may be too much for parents to handle. Sibling groups may even work together to 'overthrow' or shift the balance of power in the home away from the parents – a pathological sibling bond. This was the case in our family, as my sister often manipulated my brothers into helping her in her exploits. This could mean asking them to lie, or in one case, to hide knives in the house to help her kill my parents at night. Thankfully this never happened. Another possible difficulty with group placements is that one child may prey upon the other children, perhaps using the sibling bond to ensure compliance or silence disclosures of abuse. In such cases, ongoing but limited, supervised contact may be the better alternative to joint placement.

Following an adoption, both adopted and birth/other children need to find their place in the new family structure. The other children (and their parents) may have to deal with new behaviours in their home, the disruption of habits, and revised expectations of what having the child in the home will be like. The challenge for parents in setting appropriate boundaries becomes particularly difficult when adoptive children have severe behaviour problems. It is difficult as a birth child to grasp why another child is not responding normally towards them, such as when the new child has a reduced conscience, lies and manipulates.

Likewise, parents are often concerned about how to respond to differing levels of behaviour. There may be a sense that one child is being favoured over another because of different sets of rules for different children. When parents are discussing this, it may be helpful to consider that if one child had cancer they would do everything they could to help that child but that they would not think of giving the treatment to all of their children just to make it equal. It would only make sense to give medicine to the one that was sick. Likewise, specialized parenting strategies must be used for the children that need it, while siblings who are trustworthy and capable should be permitted greater freedoms and different opportunities.

Outsiders, including extended family, may view individualized rules as favouritism, but parents must be willing to protect their children's needs and honour each of their own strengths and weaknesses. The reality is that no matter what freedoms the 'normal' children are permitted, they are often the ones who are actually being short-changed. They often have reduced time with their parents because of the demands of the special needs child(ren); they may be victimized or have their belongings ruined; they may be socially embarrassed or ostracized by their sibling's behaviour,[3] and potentially be shunned by extended family who believe that they are being favoured by their parents. This is particularly true of mother-in-laws. Paternal grandmothers often have tense relationships with daughter-in-laws at the best of times, and when a severe behaviour child senses this they may play on the tension to gain control. This triangulation pits parents and grandparents against each other, and may place the other children in the middle. It is important for parents to recognize this and ensure that all of the children have someone – an aunt, godparent, babysitter, etc. – that will give them positive, individual attention. As well, it is helpful to find a professional who understands what it was like to live in a home with severe behaviour siblings and who can teach the child healthy coping skills and educate them about the reasons behind their sibling's behaviour.

While the 'normal' children may wish for additional attention, the behaviour disordered child may long for the 'normalcy' of other child(ren), and envy their position in the family. These children also need positive interaction, and family counsellors and psychiatrists should encourage parents not to assume that time spent consequencing, supervising, and accompanying to appointments constitutes quality, attachment-building time. No matter how severe their behaviour, these children also need to have their strengths acknowledged and experience successes. Their successes may not be the same as other children, but they should also be celebrated. Sometimes making it through a soccer game without punching another player is just as significant as winning a tournament.

The issues surrounding attachment and siblings are complex. Birth siblings, sibling separation, and adoptive/birth sibling relationships all hinge on the need for awareness of the significance of attachment – both healthy and pathological, and the need for ongoing support for families dealing with these issues. The goal of adoptive families is to build attachment at all levels and to heal the wounds of early attachment interactions. By recognizing the role that siblings play in families, parents can help both adopted and birth children to develop healthy attachments within their home and in future relationships.

[1] Levy, T. & Orlans, M. (1998). *Attachment Trauma and Healing* . CWLA Press: Washington, DC, 166.
[2] Schooler, J. (1997). When siblings are separated. *Adoptive Families, 30*(6), 14-19.
[3] Levy and Orlans, 214-215.
[4] Levy and Orlans, 166.
This article was written specifically for this book. © 2002 Society of Special Needs Adoptive Parents

The More the Merrier:
An Adoptive Parent's Perspective
by Chris Simpson

Three years ago we adopted a sibling group of two: a two year old girl named Anne* and a four year old boy named Jason. At the time we already had four biological children. Both Anne and Jason, the adopted siblings, had been diagnosed as having NAS, while the boy was diagnosed as having Partial Fetal Alcohol Syndrome (pFAS).

A Little Crazy

We first heard about adopting sibling groups through friends who had adopted two children about the same age as ours. They were pretty cute, and I have always loved kids, so we looked into it. My grandmother always said you have to be a little bit crazy to get married or have children because if you really knew everything you were in for you may not want to do it. I would include adoption in with her tidbit of insight. We really had no clue.

When we talked about it to our family, they deemed us nuts but slowly grew into the idea. And, of course, the idea of our adopted children remaining in the foster care system is not acceptable to them. They love them and brag about them along with the other grandchildren to anyone who will listen. The fact that they are a different race and skin tone has never been an issue.

When these two siblings first became part of our family we noticed that Anne was exhibiting some strange behaviours. She seemed to not understand the word "no." Also, she frequently dressed up in frilly, feminine clothes that she associated with being part of her identity. Later we learned that these behaviours were rooted in her first foster home where she seemed to have been treated as "royalty." It seemed that Anne was given many things and hadn't been taught appropriate demands. It was a surprise for her then when she moved to our home of four children (six counting her and her brother!) because she soon realized that, as with any reasonable family, there are expectations and rules.

Different Fostering Experiences

Both brother and sister had been put into foster care at birth, yet in separate foster homes. Anne's foster home felt that because she was withdrawn and a bit frail that there should be no expectations placed on her. Unfortunately she was happy and ready to meet each and every one of those nonexistent expectations and therefore was not developing, as she should. Because of the child's lack of development and lack of compliance, the decision was made to begin preplacement visits and slowly integrate Anne with her brother. The foster mom fought to stop this from happening. On what would have been Anne's first visit to her brother's foster home she was dropped off for two hours and was never picked up.

Ministry Adoption Bulletin

About five months later we saw the siblings in the Ministry adoption bulletin and requested more information. They were presented to us as two normal healthy children. One with speech delays (at this point she wasn't talking at all) and one that was performing age appropriately. I made a trip to Vancouver and met with the children's social worker and a foster parent. I was very pleased by the way the social worker "drilled" me about why our family wanted to do this.

I got the feeling that she really cared about the children and was determined to know that I didn't have just an okay home for the kids. She wanted to know that we offered the absolute best home for the kids to grow up in. One of the things she wasn't real comfortable with was the fact that we already had four children.

The funny part was that, at the time I felt like it was huge too, but now it seems like such small potatoes. Back then we were also home-schooling and that made her a little uneasy as well. After all was said and done, I guess the meeting must have gone well because if it hadn't she would have fought us "tooth and nail" to protect those kids. I appreciated that a lot. Yea for her!

Adoption Process

Plans to integrate the sibling group into our family began as soon as we said "yes" and passed our meeting with the social worker. The social worker came over to the house and began explaining the adoption process to the children. I made a book that explained, through the use of pictures from magazines, how everything would happen. I told the siblings that we were coming on a plane by cutting out a picture of a plane and pasting it into the book. I introduced each one of the kids to the other family members by telling them a few things about them such as their likes, dislikes and hobbies. I also bought two little stuffed animals and sent them along. I decorated the front cover with stickers and put their names on it. When the social worker brought it to their house they looked through it and were very interested.

Entering the Twilight Zone

A couple of weeks later we took the plane and were picked up at the airport by the social worker. She dropped us by the hotel to dispose of our luggage and then took us to the foster home to meet the children. My husband and I were pretty nervous about what would happen. When we got to the door we rang the doorbell and the door slowly opened. I seemed to recall that it creaked as it opened as though we were entering the twilight zone. It was kind of like that for us because we were both terrified. This was so different than anything we had ever done before. Then Jason squealed: "That's my new mommy and daddy!" And he exclaimed, "They brought us presents!" We got hugs from both of them and relaxed a hundred fold.

We were there for ten days before we brought them to their new home. The foster mom came back with us and stayed for three days at a hotel. That seemed to work well. However, before parents choose that route it's a good idea to make sure they have a foster mom with the maturity to look out for the best interest of the kids. This one was fabulous! It was so interesting because you could see the kids at the beginning going to her first and by the end of that ten days they had made the switch and began coming to me.

Huge Attachment Issues

When the kids came to live with us, Anne had huge attachment issues. She would single out one person and go to them and rudely reject anyone else. She had huge abandonment fears (can you blame her!). She screamed and hit lots and was not very fun to be around. She was an angel when we went to church. She wandered around like a little princess right down to using the queen wave. She melted every heart around her with her dark brown, puppy dog eyes. People would pick her up and she would snuggle in and look over their shoulders at me with a smug little look that seemed to say, "So what do you think of this?" I ended up having to go and tell people what she was up to and that it was fine for them to talk to her and give her a hug but if she pulled the "I'm so frail and can hardly lift my hand routine," they needed to send her back to us for the comfort she was obviously seeking.

At first, even though they'd spent very little time together, Jason was very protective of his biological sister. When I'd challenge Anne over one of her behaviours he would come out of nowhere and stand at her side. Before long though, once he realized that I was no threat to her, he promptly stopped this. By the way, most of Anne's behaviours have cleared up.

Different Behaviours

Jason was a little easier to handle, because he didn't possess such a strong need to fight to survive like Anne did. Also, his issues were different. He didn't follow directions well, but he persevered in most things. He was super-sensitive to temperature change. If our van had been sitting in the hot sun for a while, he would get in it and whine that he was burning up. After we opened a window he would feel that initial breeze and freak out about being freezing. He would ask you a question and when we answered it by saying: "No we will do that later because..." he would look at us blankly as if to say, "So can I?" He also had problems with sentence structure when he spoke.

Partial Fetal Alcohol Syndrome Diagnosis

I finally went to the doctor and asked that he be assessed for fetal alcohol effects. He was then diagnosed with Partial Fetal Alcohol Syndrome (pFAS). The assessment said that when he was processing information he was great, but when his brain was shut off he was "borderline retarded". Just the other day he asked me if he was allowed to go into the bathroom and use the toilet. He had a really worried look on his face. I told him absolutely any time he needed to he could use the toilet. He looked so reassured. He is now seven years old.

I used a lot of the strategies on Jason that are used in the Lovask system for autistic children. (My nephew is autistic and has Asperger's Syndrome). These strategies seemed to work well to help Jason persevere. We also used some sensory integration strategies to help him resist touching. He now seems to be a lot better at this.

Great Community Supports

The child development centre in our community was a great support to us in working out issues with Anne and Jason. Whenever we needed questions answered, they were always very happy to help. It is my understanding that we have more and faster services in our small northern town than they do in the larger centres. The people who run these services in our community do such a great job! I was a little caught off guard with the pFAS stuff. We didn't want anything like that when we started thinking about adopting. But the centre allowed us to borrow books and they offered to help in any way they could which really made a difference to us.

Good Days and Bad Days

Since we have found out about pFAS, we have learned how to be more thoughtful when we communicate ideas or instructions to Jason. He has good days and bad days and we know that. We just plan on helping him out a little more on his bad days. We don't ask him to do less and we don't allow him to behave badly on those days. If you know these things about FAS then it isn't as off-putting when a child doesn't do what you expect.

The interesting part is that we now have the kids in a private school. There are some very gifted students in that school. My boy Jason, with that "big ugly pFAS diagnosis", achieved more last year and had a higher GPA than any other student in his grade 1-4 class. He achieved the good GPA on his good days, because on his bad days it was hard for him to achieve anything at all.

Reality Talks

Prior to the sibling group being integrated into my family we did a lot of talking with my children. I was very honest with them about what things would be like. Though I do not think that all my "reality talks" could have prepared us for what we were in for. I was just really glad I was honest because it was very difficult for them. For instance, when the kids first came to live with us Jason would persist with the same question for three hours while Anne might be sobbing and drooling all over the floor because we asked her to move out of the way of the TV so others could watch it.

It also didn't help that our eight-year-old son fell and severely broke his leg four days after the kids came. He ended up in the hospital and no one could have prepared us for that. Two days after he got home in his body-cast, my daughter ended up getting emergency surgery to remove her appendix. A week after that, my aunt was brutally murdered. Two weeks after, my grandmother died. I really tried hard to prepare my children for what life would be like after the adoption. But, I didn't stand a chance at adequately preparing them for all these things.

My son with the broken leg hated the new son, mostly because Jason had called him a "donkey sheep!" Scott was furious at him for having said something so rude and dived over the edge of the bunk bed to straighten him out. That's how he broke his leg. We told him he didn't have to like Jason but he did have to be nice to him. The great part is that, now, four years later, Scott loves Jason and stands up for him. He encourages him by telling him what a great job he's doing on things.

It got better after Scott realized that Jason didn't come with a return policy and that he was here to stay. He put him through what he called "Cool School".

He said this was his plan to make Jason less embarrassing when the two went out in public. Jason was so happy to get the positive attention that he did everything Scott asked. There were positive changes in Jason's behavior and Scott felt good about that. And we were grateful that things were changing not just for the good, but the great!

Learning How to Look Deeper

So why did we decide to adopt again? Part of the reason is that we saw it work itself out the first time. Our birth kids learned compassion and they learned how to love people who didn't always respond with love. My birth kids learned so much about communicating with different kinds of people, and they learned coping skills. They learned how to look deeper, and how to put themselves aside to achieve greater goals. There were times when it wasn't fun. There were times when it really hurt my children, but it never harmed them. They now know that people can change and that everyone is worth fighting for.

When we asked the kids if they thought we should adopt again they all said: "We survived the first time. Nothing could ever be worse than that. Let's do it!" Scott was the biggest fan of our idea. Everyday for a year he asked when we would adopt. His teacher at school told me his biggest strength was that, through the adoption, he learned how to be a big brother to kids who needed one. My husband often said: "Our table is not full enough; someone is missing." Well, it turned out to be more than one person. I don't know why we did this again, but I do know that it's a good idea.

This article originally appeared in *SNAP Newsmagazine*, Vol. 18 #4, July/August 2002. © 2002 Society of Special Needs Adoptive Parents

The Odd One:
An Adoptive Sibling's Perspective
by Tanya Helton-Roberts

I have three siblings – a sister three months older, a brother 11 months younger, and another brother four years younger. Unlike many adoptive families I, as the only birth child, was the 'odd one'. This experience has given me a unique perspective on adoption and siblings, a perspective further developed when I later adopted my sister's child.

Like many siblings of severe behaviour children, I took on the role of 'parental child,'[2] being overly responsible to try to help my stressed parents and gain some sense of control in the midst of chaos. I think that I have come a long way in this area but continue to assist my siblings as they struggle with daily life choices due to their special needs. Setting appropriate boundaries on time and behaviour while acknowledging their individual needs requires a delicate balance.

When I was four years old my parents adopted a sibling group of three children, a sister (also 4) and two brothers (ages 3 years and 8 months respectively). I went from being the only child in the home to being one of four, and since my sister was three months older, technically I was no longer even the eldest. My parents had known prior to their marriage that my mother might have difficulty conceiving due to endometriosis. They felt very blessed to have a birth child and so I always knew that they viewed my birth as being very special. At the same time, both of my parents wanted to have more children. Several years before they adopted these children, they had considered adopting a family of children whose parents had been killed in a house fire. The extended family had ended up taking those children but the experience left them considering adopting a sibling group in order to keep a family together. I had always wanted siblings, particularly a baby I could help care for, so I was actively involved in the decision of our family to adopt additional children. I don't recall specific emotional preparation for the adoption but because of my mother's consistent and open communication about the process I know that I always was aware of what was going to happen next. When the call came that my parents had been selected as a home for three children from Ontario, I am told that I danced around the house singing, 'We're getting our kids, we're getting our kids!' Years later I asked my parents, 'Can't we give them back??'!

When we travelled to pick up the children, we spent several days getting to know them before returning home. I enjoyed this time. I remember the outdoor swimming pool at their foster home and the fun of finding that my sister and I had some belongings that were exactly the same (a purse, and other small items). My parents quickly noticed some abnormal behaviours but hoped that these would work out as the children adjusted to them. The trip home marked the beginning of my new role as 'parental child.' On the plane, as my mom tried unsuccessfully to stop her new baby from screaming for the duration of the ride, I sat with my new brother and sister. I was the one who noticed that my brother was eating a cinnamon bun without having removed the wax paper underneath it. He had already eaten half of it. My sister, meanwhile, would quite willingly go with anyone. As we travelled through airports I was assigned the task of holding my brother and sister's hands to ensure that they did not wander off.

Initially my sister imitated everything I did and generally was easy to get along with. We now refer to this as the honeymoon phase. What I quickly realized, however, was that she found that since she was blond and *very* cute, she could manipulate others to get anything I would want. For example, while in the grocery store soon after they came to our home, a cashier offered us all a balloon. I eyed the one green one in the container because that was my favourite colour. Knowing this, when my sister was asked which one 'the pretty girl' wanted, she chose the green one and the cashier told me I had to pick something else. As the quiet brunette, I learned that I would not get the same respect as my superficially charming sister. That day I went home and decided that green was no longer my favourite colour and that I would pick purple instead. My sister soon decided her favourite colour was yellow. It would be sixteen years before I acknowledged to myself that I could like green again.

There were many other hurts and stresses growing up with severe behaviour siblings. Physically the stress due to my sister and brother's outbursts caused me to be ill much of the time. Looking back we can laugh at the fact that our cat was on Valium during my sister's teenage years because it was so stressed it was losing the hair off its ears. I coped with the daily traumas by being the family overachiever, succeeding in school and spending most of my time reading in a corner, and the rest of the time being an assistant to my parents who desperately were seeking help and treatment for the children that most people regarded as charming and polite. It was difficult coping with holes in the wall from where my sister had punched them, and a brother with a dangerous temper who almost killed my younger brother several times. My things were stolen or wrecked, and sometimes we were in danger, so my parents put a lock on my door to protect my things and enable me to sleep safely at night.

One of the most difficult parts of growing up in this family was that my parents had little time for normal family activities. Besides the demands of supporting four children, they had to try to handle chronic chaos caused by my sister's manipulation and pathological behaviour. She managed to ruin most family occasions and outings. My parents worked very hard to develop specialized rules and rewards for each of us, as appropriate for our levels of responsibility. Others viewed this system as unfair when in reality it was the only way that could have worked. It would have been unfair to give me the same limits as my sister who would frequently lie and steal, just as it would have been unfair to expect her to carry the responsibilities I did. It was particularly hard on me that my paternal grandmother was easily conned by my sister when we visited. My sister eventually convinced her that my parents were unfair and that I was manipulative and spoiled. My Nana died refusing to speak to my Dad because of her misinformed beliefs. Being a target at home was one thing, but being punished by relatives and family friends because of my sister's lies was quite another. It meant that I, as the odd 'normal' one, received a lot of additional stress rather than support from those in my extended family.

In hindsight, I wish that there had been an aunt or other mother figure who could have been a safe confidant when my mother couldn't be and who could have given me additional support with school projects, crafts (I have been known to create quite a tornado effect on the house because of my creativity), and been a safe alternative home when the stress was too much. Even better would have been a therapist who understood what it was like to live in a home with severe behaviour siblings who could have taught me some healthy coping skills and educated me about the reasons behind their behaviour.

My sister had a child when she was 18. There is a lot of detail to how it came to pass, but the end result was that I eventually adopted this daughter when she was 2. I am amazed and honoured that when my sister knew she could not handle being a mom any more that she entrusted her child to me without hesitation. There has been so much healing for me in being able to parent a child that looks so much like my beautiful sister but who is now my child and I am able to get her the help that my sister never found.

My sister would now be diagnosed as having Reactive Attachment Disorder. My two brothers have symptoms of Fetal Alcohol Syndrome. Only one has been officially diagnosed. Interestingly, my brothers trust me to accompany them to medical and psychiatric appointments, advise them on life decisions, and mediate between them and the 'outside world' when they don't understand things.

Today our family has essentially become a family of four – my parents, my daughter and me. My brothers remain at the periphery, calling only when they want something and rarely giving anything in return. My parents and I consult on boundaries to be set, so that all of us state the same message. We offer support to them when we feel that there is an issue of health or serious injury, and set limits when we suspect we are being conned or taken advantage of. In many ways I am more than ever a parental child. As I have acquired additional professional training and expertise it has become easier for me than my parents to deal with my siblings. Sometimes this role scares me. I envision my brother when he is 89 and I am 90, and he is asking me to drive him somewhere. I hope that one day I will not have to care for my siblings. At the same time I see how far our relationship has come. I see myself able to set clear boundaries while providing support to siblings who each have their own mental health issues. I have a better understanding of why they act the way they do and what kind of help they require. I can love them as they are, without having to fix them.

When I am asked how many children are in my family, I always say four. I have no doubts that they are my siblings and in fact I consider them even more so because I chose to have them initially… and I have consciously decided to keep them.

[5] Levy, T.M. and Orlans, M. (1998). *Attachment Trauma and Healing*. CWLA Press: Washington, D.C. , 166.

This article was written specifically for this book. © 2002 Society of Special Needs Adoptive Parents

CARE OF SIBLINGS CHECKLIST

This list assumes that your adopted child has special needs that often reduces the level of equal attention the other child(ren) in your home receive. The focus is on balancing out the specialized needs of the adopted child with the normal (but also special) needs of your other children. Some ways to care for your 'normal' kids are:

- Involve your other children in the adoption process
- Give each child individual responsibilities and freedoms based on the degree of their level of dependability
- Let the siblings of a severely behavioured kid have fun away from the severely behavioured child
- Hire a counsellor for your 'normal' kids
- Allow them to lock up their belongings
- Give siblings opportunities to spend time with extended family, such as grandparents or aunts and uncles, without the other child.
- Let them build an extended network of support people, such as the families of their school friends, where they can stay during a rough week or for a weekend while you have respite care. They need respite too.
- Encourage your other children to be honest about their emotions and needs, especially in terms of the impact the other child is having on them.
- Build consequences around the special needs child's behaviour that have positive rewards for the other child (for example, when Joe does _____, the rest of us go out for ice cream while he stays with a babysitter).
- Take time to listen.

Compiled by Tanya Helton-Roberts and reprinted with permission.

disruption

FOR SOME PEOPLE, DISRUPTION
IS A DIRTY WORD. THESE
PEOPLE NEED TO CONSIDER
THAT THEY AND/OR THEIR
FAMILIES HAVE NEVER LIVED
WITH THE CHILD IN QUESTION.
    – Adoptive parent

Thoughts on Disruption

by Helen Creamore

Each one of us brings a new member into the family full of joyous expectations of growing together and truly becoming family.

While we all expect the ups and downs that are a real and natural part of that process, for some the fit is never quite right. Issues and behaviors the child brings from the past can cause severe and lasting damage within their new families. For some people, time, effort and therapy will never be enough to ensure a real sense of belonging; indeed, it feels like living in the middle of a battle zone. The stress of such a situation can be devastating to families as they struggle to cope, not only with their own feelings and questions, but also with those of people around them.

The hardest decision many people will have to make in their lives is to accept that their family cannot continue to live in emotional turmoil and that dissolving the adoption is the only alternative.

It is terribly difficult to make a decision that in many ways feels like choosing to switch off the life support that is maintaining your child. An emotional roller coaster ride of anger, guilt, sadness and despair is experienced on the way to making such a decision and it is a journey of desperation.

Much concern focuses on the thoughts and feelings of other children in the family and how they will be affected by the process. It becomes a matter of damage control -- how to escape with as little damage as possible to all the people involved.

It is vital that families forced into making such decisions are well aware of their options and have lots of support. For some, it will mean giving up their children and walking away. For others, it might mean realizing that they can no longer live together, but a relationship is possible from a greater distance.

It is often said in support groups that no one really understands like another adoptive parent. Sadly, this is often the experience in giving up a child as well. Some people have no understanding of the difficulty and pain involved in making such a decision and greatly add to the heavy burden of guilt and remorse that the relinquishing parent is already feeling. Others go to the opposite extreme and congratulate them on such a wise decision, giving no respect to the fact that they are losing a child and must grieve.

Disruption also can be a part of adoption, though hopefully one that not all of us will have to face. There is as great a need for information and support in learning to give up a child as there is in learning to parent one.

Part of the support is respecting what someone has experienced and listening to them through all phases of adoption including disruption. We would encourage anyone who is feeling in need of support to contact the SNAP office for a referral to a resource parent or the location of a support group in your area.

Nothing can ease the pain that going through such a difficult time will bring, but no one needs to struggle alone. While nothing can take the pain away, sharing it with someone who understands can make the journey a little less difficult and lonely.

This article originally appeared in the SNAP newsletter, Vol. 8 #4, Winter 1993. © 1993 Society of Special Needs Adoptive Parents

Adoption Disruption:
The Perspective of the Adoptive Parent
by Mary Runte

I recently undertook a study at the University of Lethbridge to examine the experience of adoption disruption as it is perceived by special needs adoptive parents. I started my research with the basic question: *How do parents who have adopted a special needs child experience adoption disruption?*

I spoke with parents who had adopted special needs children but either did not finalize the process or returned the child to the care of the state post-finalization. Here are some of my findings, which will likely resonate with other special needs adoptive families:

Experience of Invasiveness
The experiences of the adoption and the disruption had profound impact on the adoptive parents. The parents interviewed felt overwhelmed by the demands of the child and the decision-making process, judged by the social worker, their families and the court and fearful of the children whose behavior was unpredictable and extreme. The extreme anxiety generated by the child's behavior, the

tremendous amount of energy expended and the harshness of the legal terms of the disruption as "abandonment" and "disability of parent" were factors generating a perception of the process as being, and remaining, an invasion of privacy and ideals.

Fear

"We thought it was only a matter of time before he hurt us badly...."

The parents also discussed having experienced fear of the child whom they had adopted. All the parents reported at least one experience when the child engaged in violent behavior or threat to safety was salient. Other threats to safety included insinuations of abuse: *"She kept telling people how she would have sex with (my husband). He was terrified to be alone with her, like he needed an alibi all the time. She would later tell the worker she did it to get even."* Many continue to fear the child even if contact had been terminated for a number of years: *"He knows where I live now. We got a divorce, he knows I'm alone. I check the lock every night."*

Overwhelmed

According to all the parents interviewed, when the adoptees entered their homes, life became chaotic. Efforts to control the child's behavior failed. This resulted in an erosion of self-confidence, deterioration of energy and a perception of being out of control:

"She would have tantrums for hours at a time, we were exhausted. "

"He destroyed everything we owned... the furniture, the clothes, everything. I thought, 'I'm insane; he's insane"

"It tore us apart, I became a different person--I would cry for days at a time."

"It was like we were invaded."

These feelings of being overwhelmed persisted after the child was removed from their homes. Whereas before the child's behavior generated the greatest amount of frustration and anxiety, after the child left the home, thoughts of the child and dealing with the social workers and legal systems were most invasive:

"I thought when she left, it would end, but it didn't...I just couldn't get her out of my mind"

"I didn't want to answer the phone."

"The child left; my husband left; hell, I wanted to leave, but someone had to answer the questions."

Despite the passage of time, often years, these feelings persist:

"He'll never be gone...."

"It's been two years and I still seem to be sorting out things about this. "

"I want so much to put it behind me, but I can't."

Judged

"It was all our fault...that is what they wanted us to believe."

Each parent interviewed revealed feeling judged by others throughout the placement. According to the parents, professionals such as social workers, physicians, teachers and therapists believed that the aberrant behavior of the child evidenced deficient parenting skills and lax control of the child. All were told that they needed to "love the child more." This resulted in considerable anxiety, self-doubt and resolve to cover-up issues.

This perception of being judged persisted and intensified after the decision to disrupt was made and the child removed:

"People don't understand, they sit in judgement."

"We really lost control over our lives--there or not, he owned us. We were judged at every step."

Although the disruption process is complete, most participants revealed that they still feel judged by those aware of the events that transpired:

"I know we had to do this, but people still ask us if we did the right thing."

"I want to move to a place where no one knew him. I tried, why can't people just accept that? "

The parents in this study identified that the adoption and the disruption had a highly controlling influence. During the placement, fears for physical and personal safety dominated and added to a highly chaotic, disruptive environment that generated profound anxiety and a perception of being overwhelmed. The parents felt judged and inappropriately analyzed and became highly sensitive to this.

For most of these individuals, these feelings persisted or intensified after the child was removed. They remained fearful of reprisals and overwhelmed by the process and their own feelings of vulnerability. Antipathy regarding their decision intensified and they were often criticized for what others perceived as the ultimate failure - giving away a child. Although the disruption process is now legally complete, many of the parents continue to feel invaded as if "the enemy is still in their midst. " Many remain fearful that the child will harm them, feel burdened by the responsibility of their now irreversible decision and perceive others as condemning.

Experience of Isolation

The parents also perceived the experience as profoundly isolating. Three factors predicated this: personal shame, lack of familial support; and lack of community and structural support.

Personal Shame

The parents reported feelings of guilt and embarrassment regarding the child's behavior while he was in the home and regarding the decision to disrupt. They were uncomfortable with others being aware of the issues and found that they isolated themselves from others.

During placement, the parents felt they were somehow responsible for the child's behavior and should have had the capacity to control it. As a consequence, they were hesitant to allow people contact:

"We thought they would never come back."

"I chose to adopt. I chose my pain. I couldn't let people see me as a failure because the kid was so out of control."

Attendant to shame over the lack of control within their homes was anxiety over pervasively negative thoughts:

"You have these thoughts, like you hate yourself and that made me cut myself off even more. "

"I thought I might really lose it and I didn't want anyone around to watch."

"I was so ashamed, so depressed."

As a consequence to their shame, the parents isolated themselves. This shame intensified during the disruption phase.

"I was so happy she was gone. I felt I had to pretend to be sad 'cause only a bad person would delight in the child being gone. That made me feel a lot worse."

"The shame tore us apart. We separated. "

"I felt like I'd failed, what more can I say."

"It was like a rock around my neck."

"No one helped, but then again, I hid out."

Many of the parents interviewed continue to feel shame regarding the disruption, although coupled with resignation over the event, the sentiment is less intense:

"Sometimes I'd wake up crying."

"I'm scared about what to tell a new man in my life, I don't want him thinking I would do this to any child."

"I'm sure I did the right thing, but at the same time I keep thinking ''if I had done this..."

"Sometimes I lie and pretend I never have had kids."

Lack of Familial Support:

Lack of familial support was and remains to be a dominant factor in the parents' perception of isolation. From initial questioning of the adoption to "horror" and "disgust" at the child's behavior to "shock" and "doubt" about the disruption, the parents felt unsupported by their families. Many experienced divorce and those whose marriages remained intact reported intense stress on the relationships:

"We turned on each other."

"If he had helped more it would have been easier."

"I didn't want to come home anymore, who would?"

The extended family was perceived as unsupportive:

"My mother used the old line: 'you made your bed, now sleep in it.'"

"I tried to get babysitting help - no one would."

During the disruption, support remained scarce:

"No one wanted to listen."

"My mother told me I shouldn't have quit."

Most continue to feel unsupported by family whom they expressed either blamed them for the disruption or cannot understand their continued grief and shame:

"Last Christmas I said 'I wonder how the child is doing?' My sister said I am obsessed."

"My mother told a friend that I might as well have killed her only grandchild."

"My ex-husband still won't talk about it."

The lack of familial support is apparently very painful to the parents in this study.

Lack of Community/Structural Support

The parents in this study reported intensive efforts to locate support from community and government. These searches were, apparently, ineffectual. If services were accessed, they were characterized as unhelpful, invasive or too late:

"The counsellor told my husband that it was all my fault.

"After we told the social worker we wanted to disrupt, she offered a child care worker."

"I tried to get some help, but no one had any answers. Maybe there weren't any."

During the disruption, the parents identified a complete lack of community or structural supports. Family therapy services would only work with the complete family or with the parents if they committed to working towards reconciliation. Social workers identified that the child was now the client, not the family.

"It was like we committed a terrible sin, no one would come near us."

"We felt shunned by our church."

"The social worker never asked how I was."

The focus during the disruption was on the child, which caused some parents to feel resentful:

"It was always (the child), what about us?"

"It was hard on me too, you know?"

Interestingly, four parents identify receiving support from community services in the post disruption phase which remain helpful. The remainder identified that this interview was their first opportunity to talk to someone about the disruption and what it meant to them. Those who have identified supports reveal:

"The church is helpful; we pray together. "

"The counsellor really helped me feel better about my decision."

"I found a group I can really say things to."

Those parents who identified community supports as still lacking report:

"I've given up on counsellors."

"Do-gooders who do no good. I don't trust anyone anymore. "

Support from family or community services is either lacking or unable to meet the needs of many of these individuals. The difficulty in accessing services is further compounded by what appears to be a pattern of self-isolating behavior generated by shame. Their families appears not to understand the issues faced by these parents or are experiencing their own grief. During the placement, services were not made available, were prohibitively expensive or were ineffective. After the decision to disrupt, many services were withdrawn because of limited mandates. In the post-disruption phase, some parents have been able to foster support, although most of the participants continue to perceive themselves as isolated and not understood.

Experience of Ignorance

The parents interviewed for this study identified a lack of accurate information as problematic during and after the adoption. Often information was not made available for reasons of confidentiality or because of ignorance on the part of professionals themselves. The parents also reported that they felt deceived by the professionals involved in the adoption and the care of the child. Regarding the dissemination of information by professionals, particularly social workers, the parents perceived that they were mislead, deceived or actively lied to:

"It was all on the records that we were entitled to."

"I think he just wanted her off his caseload."

"I thought about suing for fraud."

During the disruption, the parents also perceived deceit on the part of the professionals. This was highly distressing to them and resulted in feelings of distrust, resentment and anger:

"They would say one thing and do another."

"I felt like a criminal with no rights."

The parents volunteered that they continue to feel deceived and that neither time nor distance has mitigate the deleterious impact of this:

"I still feel so angry."

"I keep trying to get them to tell the truth but they won't."

"If we had known the truth, things may have been different. Who elected them god?"

Unavailability of Information

The participants report difficulties in obtaining information about their child and the adoption and disruption processes due to unavailability of information or difficulty in access. Information about the children was sealed by the state; that was highly frustrating to the adoptive parents who felt that they had a right to information on their child's history:

"The records were sealed... it was frustrating. There was stuff no one knew, like that the mother was an alcoholic."

Information regarding the special needs of their children was often scarce. In addressing the problems encountered with their children, the parents sought information and guidance. Often they were told that:

"...no one knows."

"They are just beginning to do research on that, but there is nothing now. "

This was frustrating and led to further difficulties as techniques to modify behavior were attempted and subsequently aborted due to negligible impact. Often services were not available in their communities, or the expense of access prohibitive, or they preferred access to services outside their local for reasons of anonymity.

The parents' isolation and anxiety was compounded during the disruption by a lack of information about the process and about their rights and obligations. Perhaps because of the rarity of disruption, services seemed ill-equipped to assist these individuals.

"We were shocked when they never let us say good-bye. "

"I had no idea what was going on, no one seemed to."

"I didn't fit in with adoptive or parent support groups. I didn't fit in anywhere. I had to explain what disruption meant to the counsellor. Some help!"

All the parents expressed continued concern regarding not having accurate or complete information. Universally, they revealed that education and accurate information about their child, special needs, and the process would have made the experience less threatening and isolating and may have impacted the outcome.

"I don't think having known would have ultimately changed things, but I sure would have felt better and maybe I could have helped (the child) more."

"I made a lot of mistakes I feel bad about. I didn't know any better. The information just wasn't there".

"I had no idea what I was getting into."

Resignation

As a function of time and distance, the parents appear to have resolved some of the ambivalence evident in the earlier stages of the adoption and disruption. In retrospect, all the parents identified that the disruption was inevitable:

"It was impossible from the beginning. "

"No one could live with the child."

"Given who we were and who she is, it was a bad match from day one. It could never be."

They have also formed clear impressions of who or what was ultimately responsible for the dissolution of the relationship.

"If the worker had told me the truth, I would never have gone through with it."

"The child could have made it work. He never wanted to be in a family."

"If the birth mom had looked after him, none of this would have happened."

"If my husband had supported us and not left, we would have made it."

"It was my fault... it had to be, I was the mother."

During the debriefing, much time was spent with the participants validating their pain and assuring them that I did not view them as "evil", "horrible" or "pathetic." Although some of the parents identified that they are "getting on with life", it appears that their pain remains and healing is yet to be complete. Emotions ranging from grief and profound sadness to resentment and hostility were expressed, often in confusing and explosive patterns.

Implications for Practice

It was clear from the data that the adoption and disruption processes were highly distressing to the parents. The participants identified a lack of effectual supports. More community-based services are indicated as well as a need for a higher profile for existing resources. Family counselling and peer support may have mitigated the erosion of confidence and isolation experienced during the placement and thus impacted the disruption. During disruption and post-disruption, emphasis was focused on the child, often to the exclusion of the relinquishing parents. Specialized services sensitive to disruption are vital to assist the parents to integrate this experience.

Support agencies should consider expanding their support group base as well as improving efforts to inform all prospective adoptive parents of their services. Support throughout the process appears elemental to adoption. Lack of familial support was also identified by the participants as contributory to the isolation and disparity of the experience. Public awareness of adoption and special needs may alter the perception of parental responsibility for aberrant behavior and thus encourage others to be supportive. Involving extended family in support groups and educational services is indicated.

The invasiveness of the child's behavior indicates a need for review of support services particularly a need for family counselling and respite support. The parents' fear of the children's abusive behavior indicates a need for further intensive intervention. Educating adoption workers, adoptive parents, physicians, teachers and counsellors regarding the impact of abuse and/or psychiatric disorders is critical. A prevailing attitude of "love will cure anything" is unhelpful and in fact harmful.

The parents often expended their financial resources in seeking treatment for their child. Assisted adoptions, with financial support for treatment, should be offered more readily and requests thereof should not factor against prospective adoptive parents being considered for placement.

Respite care or short-term foster care is prohibitively expensive. Placing a child voluntarily in the care of others should be more feasible. Short-term care agreements may offer parents and child opportunities to distance from the situation before the irreversible decision to disrupt is made. The parents' evidence of profound exhaustion delineates the need for preventative relief.

Lack of information and deception has abstruse implications. Open adoptions, where ongoing contact is offered with birth parents, and adoption orientation/ training are now offered in many Canadian provinces. These new dimensions of the adoption process may facilitate communication. Education regarding special needs is also indicated. Critical in adoption is the dissemination of accurate information. Although the participants in this study revealed a dearth of information, the need for accuracy must predominate over amount. A careful analysis of educational programs should be undertaken, assessing material and curriculum for accuracy and evaluating effectiveness before extending the scope of the programs.

Implications for Adoptive Parents
I ended my interviews and the debriefing sessions by asking the participants: "If there is anything you would like another adoptive parent considering disruption to know, what would it be?" I will end this article with their "advice from the battlefield":

"Talk about it. Talk about how you feel; don't stop talking or you will stop feeling."

"Find a support group. If you prefer, contact a parent volunteer on the phone for some free and anonymous support. Keep trying until you find someone who will listen."

"Talk to people considering adoption. You don't have to give them your horror story, but you should tell them what information to ask for, like the birth parents' drug use, and where to get information and support."

"Sometimes, some parts of the problem, were really your fault. Acknowledge when you made mistakes. But some parts aren't your fault. Don't forget that. It isn't always your fault."

"Try to keep your supports around you. Don't overuse any one support, but don't under use them either. Some friends really do want to listen."

"People can be jerks; only listen to people who really care about you."

"The battlefield is ugly; think about it. Get some help first."

"Don't give up on loving and having a family. Just because one adoption isn't successful doesn't mean that you are forever incapable of love."

This article was adapted specifically for this book, from the author's full report *Adoption Disruption: the Perspective of the Adoptive Parent.* ©2002 Society of Special Needs Adoptive Parents

How to Deal with Disruption

1. Do not go through the crisis alone! Remember, it is never too early or too late to reach out. If your instincts tell you that something is worsening in your adoptive family relationships, and your normal approaches are not working, go for help. Even if yours is a chronic set of problems you are entitled to information and assistance.

Connect with your placement agency if there is one, to see what resources they presently have to offer. (They also need to know what is going on with families in the years after placement, in order to provide proper services to new families.)

One of your best resources for help is another parent who has been through this same type of crisis. Look for local parent self-help groups, school guidance counsellors, church counselors, community or hospital mental health resources.

You may not be the first adoptive parent to go to your parent group for help. See what networks have been established. If none exist, you may want to establish links with other adoptive families in crisis.

Get legal advice if you need it. Be clear about your current and future financial and legal responsibilities.

2. Sort out the facts! Figure out if the problem is a "kid problem" or an adoption problem. Talk to your friends about the behavior of their adolescents to make a better judgment about problems in your family. You may be dealing with fairly typical "teenage-ittis."

3. Look for patterns! Take another look at your child's family background and placement history to see how these current problems may have emerged. Problems often follow patterns. It is urgent that adoptive parents have access to the child's complete history before finalization, including early life history. Although many families tend to discard material about their children after the adoption, this critically important information should be saved with other important family papers for use if needed in later crisis counseling.

4. Keep a log of major happenings! This can prove useful to protect yourself if your actions are questioned, and to help diagnose problems which may be obscure or hidden.

5. Avoid over-reacting or under-reacting! Be careful in assessing your child's problems and the threat to your family. You can seriously under-estimate or over-estimate the danger when the situation gets explosive. You can also become immobilized by guilt.

6. Use effective helpers! Only use therapists familiar with placement dynamics. If there do not seem to be appropriate mental health facilities in your area, investigate how other families have organized to solve their own problems.

7. Be open to your child's point of view! Are you both talking and listening? Is there room for your opinion and your child's opinion at your table? Make sure that your child knows where you stand on these important issues: his/her past history, life experiences, current behavior, and, most important, your commitment.

8. Be the parent! Do not relinquish custody as the price of help. Do not conclude that the easy way is necessarily the best way. You and your child have a considerable investment in each other. As your child's legal parent, you are in the strongest position to make decisions, find resources, demand assistance, find your way out of difficulties, and help other families in the same circumstances.

This tip list originally appeared in the booklet *Adoption Disruption* (Adoptive Parents Association of Alberta, 1988). It is reprinted here with permission of APA Alberta.

redefining
family

FAMILIES CHANGE AND REMAIN
THE SAME. WHY ARE OUR
NAMES FOR HOME SO SLOW TO
CATCH UP TO THE TRUTH OF
WHERE WE LIVE?

– Barbara Kingsolver

Celebrating Diversity in Adoption

by Sara Graefe

Canadian society is a rich tapestry, woven together with men and women with diverse cultural backgrounds, ages, races, marital status, sexual orientation, religious affiliation, physical abilities—to name but a few of the differences that distinguish us as individuals and groups.

For people of the 90s, diversity is a familiar concept. *Diversity, equity, multiculturalism* and *affirmative action* have effectively become buzzwords of the decade. Both governments and the private sector have shown a commitment to combating prejudice and discrimination, while taking steps towards including *all* people and celebrating our differences—be it in the work force, the schools, or society at large.

Being on the Outside

When we talk about diversity, we're referring to variations from the majority or dominant groups that exist in our society. As adoptive parents of a special needs child, for example, you vary from the majority both by being a family built through adoption, and by parenting a child with extraordinary needs. In these two facets of your life, you experience day to day what it is like to be *other*—an outsider. After adopting your child, you likely discovered very quickly that the world around you—apart from being designed for people *without* disabilities—assumes that family means *birth family,* simply by default. This is a typical experience for a member of any minority group—having one's unique needs and experiences excluded by the majority, due to prejudice, intolerance, or, most commonly, simple lack of awareness.

In a society which strives to include all people as active participants, the dominant culture has the responsibility to foster an environment in which differences and diversity are not only tolerated, but appreciated and celebrated. Members of minority groups can greatly help the cause by making themselves visible, speaking out against discrimination, and refusing to settle for less. That's why raising awareness around adoption and special needs issues is so important—be it by lobbying government, participating in an Adoption Month event, or educating your child's teacher. In promoting adoption awareness, we're celebrating our differences while defining common ground: we're reminding ourselves and the rest of the world that families formed by adoption are a distinct, vibrant fabric in society—while at the same time asserting that we are just as much a "family" as any other.

Differences Within our Own Community

While it's important to promote the visibility of the adoption community in society at large, it's also crucial to celebrate the diversity that exists *within* the community itself. The stereotyped image of "adopted family"—which is not surprisingly rooted in the experience of the dominant culture—is the replication of the nuclear family unit through adoption, i.e. Mom and Dad and their adopted kids. Certainly this is one possibility—but there are also many alternatives, as families brought together by adoption are as diverse, complicated and rich as family constellations built in any other way. Adoptive parents can include single parents, same sex couples, and older adults, who are sometimes grandparents adopting their birth grandchildren. There are transracial adoptive families—some built through international adoption, others through domestic, cross-cultural adoption. There are white families raising aboriginal children, as well as aboriginal families who adopt within the First Nations community. There are step parents who adopt their partner's children from a previous relationship. There are relatives caring for kith and kin. There are children in open adoptions who have close ties with both their birth and adoptive parents. There are children in adopted families whose lifestyles and values conflict with those of their adopted parents. The list can go on and on. Each variation merits acceptance and celebration as an adoptive family in its own right.

Do you feel yourself reacting to any of these examples? It is important to be aware of your own attitudes and prejudices—of where you draw a line in terms of your own tolerance. We recognize that accepting and celebrating diversity is demanding and challenging, and takes years—perhaps even a lifetime—of unlearning internalized beliefs and stereotypes.

BC's New Adoption Act

The challenging nature of these issues came to the fore during consultation around British Columbia's new *Adoption Act*, which was implemented in 1996. This progressive piece of legislation was heralded around the world for breaking ground in many areas. While most of the media attention was focused on the unsealing of records, it is also significant that, for the first time in this province, the legislation formally recognizes diversity in adoption.

The entire *Act* is founded on the principle of providing "new and permanent family ties through adoption, giving paramount consideration in every respect to the child's best interests." By "family ties," the *Act* includes a whole range of family constellations, the bottom line being that each particular placement is in the best interests of that particular child.

Basically, the law enables one adult or two adults jointly to apply to adopt. Under the previous legislation, only single people and legally married couples were eligible to adopt, which excluded common-law and gay and lesbian couples. An individual could not apply to adopt a partner's child from a previous relationship, even when such an arrangement could provide the child with more security and stability. The direct placement option and the *Act's* commitment to preserving kinship ties facilitates adoption by grandparents or other birth relatives.

The new *Act* also addresses some significant cultural issues. For example, it stresses that the importance of preserving the child's cultural identity must be considered when determining an aboriginal child's best interests. When an aboriginal child is to be adopted, the Ministry or licensed agency must notify the child's Band or identified aboriginal community before placement and consult with them about planning. The new legislation also recognizes an adoption carried out under the custom of an aboriginal community or Indian band as being the same as adoptions carried out under the *Act*. Also, the regulation of international adoptions for the first time recognizes that some BC families come together through transcountry, often transracial adoption, and that certain standards are required to ensure, once again, that placement meets the best needs of the child.

Needless to say, debate around these issues during the consultation process was heated indeed. Each party at the table brought with them their own values, beliefs, prejudices, and internalized stereotypes. As soon as the government made it clear that one hundred percent consensus from the community was required for the legislation to proceed at all, a remarkable thing happened. People were able to set aside their differences, in some cases agreeing to disagree, in order to come together as a unified community to back legislation that more accurately reflects the realities and concerns of all members of the adoption circle.

Celebrating Diversity

SNAP is committed to serving all adoptive families, no matter how constructed, and supports any placement that is in the best interests of the child. In the spirit of the current times and the new *Adoption Act,* SNAP wishes to acknowledge and celebrate the diversity that exists within our community.

This article is excerpted from a longer piece that originally appeared in the SNAP newsletter, Vol. 14#2, Summer 1998. © 1998 Society of Special Needs Adoptive Parents

Redefining the Family through Adoption
by Lissa Cowan

As an organization that was founded for and by adoptive parents sharing stories and experiences (around a kitchen table), SNAP has always encouraged parents with children who have special needs to advocate on behalf of their children and on behalf of themselves as individuals who are vital to a child's well-being, personal growth and success in life. As all adoptive parents of children who have special needs know, advocating isn't easy. There are those in society who might feel that the issues around special needs simply aren't important enough, that early testing is a waste of taxpayer's money, invisible disabilities don't count (are in fact, *invisible*), and education doesn't matter because some children *never* learn. Getting the necessary support from family, friends, teachers, community, and government is often an uphill battle. Parent duties such as educating a child's teacher, lobbying government, and writing a letter to a local community group seem never-ending.

Being Counted, Fitting in
For parents with children who have special needs, feeling included, and being counted, is as important as a child's basic need to fit in at school and be accepted by his or her peers. We ALL feel the need to fit in. Yet, what about when it comes to definitions of family? Just what is this definition of family we're supposed to fit into? And if our families aren't included in the pre-established idea of what a family is supposed to be, how are we to fit in?

Fostering Openness
Launching an issue on redefining family goes hand-in-hand with SNAP's commitment to strive to include all individuals as active members of society, which means supporting configurations of families in so far as they promote the best interests of the child. By being inclusive we hope to foster an environment in which differences and diversity are appreciated and celebrated. Whether it's a non-nuclear adoptive family such as a single parent household, an adoptive parent who is also the child's grandmother, or, a traditional two-parent household,

these manifestations all come under the definition of family.

Meaning of Family

If we look at the origin of the word family, dating back to the fifteenth century, we find that the word means a group of individuals living under one roof; a group of people united by certain convictions or a common affiliation. A current designation gives us a more precise meaning of a group in society traditionally consisting of two parents rearing their own or adopted children. In the past, most Canadians defined families as consisting of a mother, father and 2.2 more children. Although there have always been households that were more multigenerational than nuclear (with an assortment of grandparents, relatives, in-laws and siblings), we tend to envision the family, in historical terms, as being a smaller unit. Adoptive families took their cue from this same model of the nuclear family. Today our perception of what family is has expanded considerably and often challenges past and current beliefs of what family *is*. We no longer refer to the nuclear family as the model around which families should be based. These days there are multiracial families, blended families, grandparents raising their grandchildren, single-parent families, lesbian and gay families. The list goes on. So, how does adoption fit in to this growing scenario? BC's new Adoption Act which was implemented in 1996 affirms the importance of diversity in adoption. The Act provides "new and permanent family ties through adoption, giving paramount consideration in every respect to the child's best interests."

This article is excerpted from a longer piece that originally appeared in the SNAP newsmagazine, Vol. 17#4, July/August 2001. © 2001 Society of Special Needs Adoptive Parents

cultural
issues

MY PARENTS HAVE ALWAYS
TRIED TO STRENGTHEN MY
SELF-ESTEEM. THANKS TO MY
MOTHER, WHO MUST HAVE
TOLD ME THE STORY OF HAITI
AT LEAST A DOZEN TIMES, I'LL
NEVER FORGET WHO MY
ANCESTORS ARE. THANKS TO
MY FATHER, I KNOW I'M AT
HOME IN MONTREAL.

– Magda Exentus-Delorme

—— Transracial & Transcultural Adoption ——

Transracial or transcultural adoption means placing a child who is of one race or ethnic group with adoptive parents of another race or ethnic group. In the United States these terms usually refer to the placement of children of colour or children from another country with Caucasian adoptive parents.

People choose to adopt transracially or transculturally for a variety of reasons. Fewer young Caucasian children are available for adoption in the United States than in years past, and some adoption agencies that place Caucasian children do not accept singles or applicants older than 40. Some prospective adoptive parents feel connected to a particular race or culture because of their ancestry or through personal experiences such as travel or military service. Others simply like the idea of reaching out to children in need, no matter where they come from.

Adoption experts have different opinions about this kind of adoption. Some say that children available for adoption should always be placed with a family with at least one parent of the same race or culture as the child. This is so the child can develop a strong racial or cultural identity. These people say that adoption agencies with a strong commitment to working with families of colour and that are flexible in their procedures are very successful in recruiting "same race" families. Other experts say that race should not be considered at all when selecting a family for a child. To them, a loving family that can meet the needs of a particular child is all that matters. Still others suggest that after an agency works very hard to recruit a same-race family for a certain period of time but does not find one, the child should be placed with a loving family of any race or culture who can meet the child's needs.

Despite the experts' differing opinions, there are many transracial and transcultural families, and many more will be formed. If you are or wish to be a parent in one of these families, this fact sheet will help you by answering two questions: (1) What should you do to prepare for adopting a child of a race or culture different from yours? And (2) After adoption, what can you do to help your child become a stable, happy, healthy individual, with a strong sense of cultural and racial identity?

How You Can Prepare for a Transracial or Transcultural Adoption

Preparation for adoption is important for anyone thinking about adopting a child. It is even more important for parents considering transracial or transcultural adoption because it will introduce you to all aspects of adoptive parenthood, help you learn about adoption issues, and help you identify the type of child you wish to parent. Any adoption agency that conducts and supervises transracial or transcultural adoptions should provide this important service. If you are undertaking an independent adoption, you should seek counselling and training in these areas. You should also read as many articles and books as you can on the subject.

The following sections describe some issues to consider as you prepare for a transracial or transcultural adoption.

Examine Your Beliefs and Attitudes About Race and Ethnicity

While you may think you know yourself and your family members very well, it is important to examine your beliefs and attitudes about race and ethnicity before adopting a child of another race or culture. Try to think if you have made any assumptions about people because of their race or ethnic group. There are two reasons for this exercise: (1) to check yourself--to be sure this type of adoption will be right for you; and (2) to prepare to be considered "different."

When you adopt a child of another race or culture, it is not only the child who is different. Your family becomes a "different" family. Some people are comfortable with difference. To them, difference is interesting, wonderful, and special. Other people are not so comfortable with difference, and are scared by it. Thus, some friends, family members, acquaintances, and even strangers will rush to your side to support you, while others may make negative comments and stare. During the pre-adoption phase, you should think about how you will respond to the second group in a way that will help your child feel good about himself or herself. (We'll give you some ideas a little later.)

When your child is young, an extra hug and a heart-to-heart talk might be all it takes to help him or her through a difficult situation. While the hugs and the heart-to-heart talks never stop, as your child gets older, you and your child will need more specific coping skills to deal with the racial bias you might face together as a family. Are you ready to fully understand these issues and help your family deal with whatever happens?

Think About Your Lifestyle

Before considering a transracial or transcultural adoption, take a look at your current lifestyle. Do you already live in an integrated neighbourhood, so that your child will be able to attend an integrated school? If not, would you consider moving to a new neighbourhood? Do you already have friends of different races and ethnic groups? Do you visit one another's homes regularly? Do you attend multicultural festivals? Do you enjoy different kinds of ethnic foods? How much of a leap would it be to start doing some of these things?

It is important for children of colour growing up with Caucasian parents to be around adults and children of many ethnic groups, and particularly, to see adult role models who are of the same race or ethnic group. These people can be their friends, teach them about their ethnic heritage, and as they mature, tell them what to expect when they are an adult in your community. Can you make these types of relationships available for your child?

Consider Adopting Siblings

It is always good for siblings to be adopted together. It is no different in the case of transracial or transcultural adoption. Siblings who are adopted together have the security of seeing another person in the family who looks like them. They are able to bring a part of their early history and birth family with them to their adoptive family, which may help them adjust better. And with internationally adopted children, being together might mean they will be able to keep up their native language.

Let's say, then, that you have examined your beliefs and attitudes about race and ethnicity. You have thought about your lifestyle and considered adopting siblings. You are sure you want to adopt a child from another race or culture. What comes next?

How You Can Help Your Child To Become a Stable, Happy, Healthy Individual With a Strong Sense of Racial or Cultural Identity

The seven parenting techniques listed below are compiled from books and articles on adoption and by interviewing experts in transracial and transcultural adoption. Some of these "techniques" are common sense and apply to all adopted children. However, with transracially or transculturally adopted children, these techniques are especially important.

Parents in a transracial or transcultural family should do the following:

- Become intensely invested in parenting;
- Tolerate no racially or ethnically biased remarks;
- Surround yourselves with supportive family and friends;

- Celebrate all cultures;
- Talk about race and culture;
- Expose your child to a variety of experiences so that he or she develops physi cal and intellectual skills that build self-esteem; and
- Take your child to places where most of the people present are from his or her race or ethnic group.

The next sections provide more information on these techniques.

Become Intensely Invested in Parenting

Dr. Larry Schreiber, former president of the North American Council on Adoptable Children (NACAC), an umbrella organization for a large number of adoptive parent support groups in the United States and Canada, wrote a column about his transracial adoption experience in the Winter 1991 issue of *Adoptalk*, the NACAC newsletter. He characterizes transracial parenting as a "roller coaster of exaggerated parenting." As a Caucasian adoptive father of African-American, Latino, Korean, Cambodian, East Indian, and Caucasian children, he describes transracial parenting as the most joyous experience of his life. He admits that he doesn't really know what it is like to endure the racially-biased name-calling that his children have experienced, but he was always there for them when they needed to be comforted and to help them get through those difficult times.

Dr. Schreiber says that transracial parenting has both complicated and enriched his life. He had to work hard to help his children develop their cultural pride and self-esteem in a world that sometimes does not understand or is unkind to people from different cultures.

However, he believes his children did overcome these difficulties and were able to develop positive cultural identities, mostly because of the help his family received from adoptive parent support groups and from other adults of the same cultural groups as his children.

Ms. Ro Anne Elliott is another experienced adoptive parent in an interracial family who has written about the importance of investing in parenting. An African-American woman, Ms. Elliott encourages parents in transracial families to empower themselves and believe strongly that their family belongs together. She writes, "You need the firm knowledge in your heart and in your mind that you are the best parent for your children. This empowerment is key, since you can't parent well if you don't feel confident, competent, and entitled to do so." She says that being in an interracial family is the opportunity of a lifetime, allowing you to embark on "a journey of personal transformation, growing in your ability to nurture your children along the way. This involves an alert awareness of difference and optimistic expectation that cultural differences among us will lead to rewarding personal connections and friendships."

The message, then, is that transracial parenting is not laid-back, catch-as-catch-can parenting. According to these two experienced adoptive parents, the demands are great, but so are the rewards.

Tolerate No Racially or Ethnically Biased Remarks

As adoptive parents in an interracial or intercultural family, you should refuse to tolerate any kind of racially or ethnically biased remark made in your presence. This includes remarks about your child's race or ethnic group, other races and ethnic groups, or any other characteristic such as gender, religion, age and physical or other disability. Make it clear that it is not okay to make fun of people who are different, and it is not okay to assume that all people of one group behave the same way. Teach your children how to handle these remarks, by saying, for instance, "I find your remark offensive. Please don't say that type of thing again," or "Surely you don't mean to be critical, you just don't have experience with..." or "You couldn't be deliberately saying such an inappropriate comment in front of a child. You must mean something else."

Try to combat the remarks while giving the person a chance to back off or change what has been said. This way you will teach your child to stand up to bias without starting a fight—which could put your child at risk. In addition, by being gracious and giving others a chance to overcome their bias/ignorance, you can help to change their beliefs and attitudes over time. Positive exchanges about race will always be more helpful than negative ones.

Surround Yourselves With Supportive Family and Friends

While you were thinking about adopting transracially or transculturally, did you find some people in your circle of family and friends who were especially supportive of your plans to become a multicultural family? If so, surround yourself with these people! In addition, seek out other adoptive families, other transracial or multicultural families, and other members of your child's racial or ethnic group. You will be surprised by how helpful many people will want to be, whether it is to show you how to cook an ethnic dish or teach you some words in their language. According to Ms. Ro Anne Elliott, "You need a supportive community comprised of many races–those who will be role models and provide inspiration, those who will stimulate your thinking, those who fill your desire for cultural diversity, and those who will challenge you in constructive and respectful ways."

Celebrate All Cultures

As a multicultural family, you should value all cultures. Teach your child that every ethnic group has something worthwhile to contribute, and that diversity is this country's and your family's strength. For example, you might give your Korean daughter a Korean doll, but you might also start a collection for her of dolls of many different racial and ethnic groups. If your child is from South America, go to the Latino festival in your town, but also visit the new Native-American art exhibit, eat at the Greek fair, and dance at the Polish dance hall. Incorporate the art, music, drama, literature, clothing, and food of your child's ethnic group and others into your family's daily life. Invite friends from other cultures to celebrate your holidays and special occasions, and attend their events as well.

The area of religion brings up special concerns. You may wish to take your child to a place of worship in your community where most of the members are from the same ethnic group as your child; for example, you could bring your East Indian child to a Hindu temple or your Russian child to a Russian Orthodox church. What an opportunity to meet people of his ethnic group, find adult role models, and learn the customs of his heritage! However, before you do this, be sure you could be supportive if your child decides to practice that religion. If you have your heart set on raising your child in your own family's religion—one that is different from the religion practised in the place of worship you will visit—tell your child that the visit is for a cultural, not religious, purpose or perhaps decide not to visit at all. Practically speaking, you can impose your religious practice on your child for only a few years. As an adult, your child will ultimately decide whether to practice any religion at all, and whether it will be one that people of his or her heritage often practice, your family's religion, or yet another one that he or she chooses.

While it is important to teach your child that differences among people are enriching, it is also important to point out similarities. One expert suggests that in an adoptive family the ratio should be two similarities for each difference. For instance, to a young child you might say, "Your skin is darker than Daddy's, but you like to play music, just like he does, and you both love strawberry ice cream." As much as you want to celebrate your child's distinctive features, he or she also needs to feel a sense of belonging in the family.

Talk About Race and Culture

How has race or culture defined you? What is life like for a Latino person in America? What is life like for a Caucasian person? An African-American person? An Asian person? How are persons of different ethnic groups treated by police officers, restaurant employees, social organizations, or government agencies? What do you think about interracial dating and marriage? As a multicultural family, you need to address these and other racial matters.

Talk about racial issues, even if your child does not bring up the subject. Use natural opportunities, such as a television program or newspaper article that talks about race in some way. Let your child know that you feel comfortable discussing race–the positive aspects as well as the difficult ones. On the positive side, a child of a certain race may be given preferential treatment or special attention. On the other hand, even a young child needs to know that while your family celebrates difference, other families do not know many people who are different. These families are sometimes afraid of what they do not know or understand, and may react at times in unkind ways. It can be difficult to deal with such issues, especially when your child is young and does not yet know that some adults have these negative feelings, but you have to do it. You will help your child become a strong, healthy adult by preparing him or her to stand up in the face of ignorance, bias, or adversity.

Stand behind your children if they are the victim of a racial incident or have problems in your community because of the unkind actions of others. This does not mean you should fight their battles for them, but rather support them and give them the tools to deal with the blows the world may hand them. Confront racism openly. Discuss it with your friends and family and the supportive multicultural community with which you associate. Rely on adults of colour to share their insights with both you and your child. Above all, if your child's feelings are hurt, let him talk about the experience with you, and acknowledge that you understand.

Ms. Lois Melina, a Caucasian adoptive parent of Korean children and a noted adoption writer, lists five questions for you to ask your child to help him or her deal with problem situations:

- What happened?
- How did that make you feel?
- What did you say or do when that happened?
- If something like that happens again, do you think you will deal with it the same way?
- Would you like me to do something?

It is important to leave the choice of your involvement up to your child. This way, you show that you are available to help, but also that you have confidence in your child's ability to decide when your help is needed.

Expose Your Child to a Variety of Experiences so that He or She Develops Physical and Intellectual Skills That Build Self-Esteem

This parenting technique is important for all children, but it is specially important for children of colour. Children of colour need every tool possible to build their self-esteem. While society has made strides in overcoming certain biases and forms of discrimination, there remain many subtle and not-so-subtle colour or race-related messages that are discouraging and harmful to young egos. Be alert to negative messages that are associated with any race or culture. Point them out as foolish and untrue. Emphasize that each person is unique and that we all bring our own individual strengths and weaknesses into the world. Frequently compliment your child on his or her strengths. Draw attention to the child's ability to solve math problems, play ball, dance, play a musical instrument, ride a bike, take photographs, perform gymnastics, or any other activity that increases confidence. Self-esteem is built on many small successes and lots of acknowledgement. A strong ego will be better able to deal with both the good and the bad elements of society.

As your child gets older, keep in touch with his or her needs: this might mean buying him or her a few of the "in" clothes or enrolling him or her on the popular teams. Stay in tune with your child's natural skills and talents, and do whatever you can to help him or her develop them at each age.

Take Your Child to Places Where Most of the People Present are from His or Her Race or Ethnic Group

If you bring your African-American child to an African-American church, or your Peruvian child to a Latino Festival, your child will experience being in a group in which the number of people present of his ethnic group is larger than the number of Caucasians present. Adoptive family support group events are other places where this might happen. Children usually enjoy these events very much. If you adopted a young child from another country, you might consider taking a trip to that country when the child is older and can understand what the trip is all about. Many adoptive families who take such a trip find it to be a wonderful learning experience.

Another benefit of such an experience is that it might be one of the few times when you feel what it is like to be in the minority. This will increase your awareness and ability to understand your child's experience as a minority individual.

Identity Needs of Children Placed Cross-Racially/Culturally

by Robert O'Connor

The qualities necessary to enhance the normal development of any child in placement, these needs are:

- To live in an environment that provides the child an opportunity to participate in positive experiences with their culture, religion, and language.
- For association with same race adult and peer role models and relationships on an ongoing basis.
- For environmental experiences that teaches survival, problem solving, and coping skills which give the child a sense of racial and ethnic pride.
- For a parent who can understand the child's life and daily relationship to racial and cultural differences and who can respond to those experiences with acceptance, understanding, and empathy.
- For a parent who accepts and can help the child accept the child's racial and cultural ancestry and can comfortably share knowledge and information about the child's racial and cultural ancestry with the child.
- For the child to have adults around them who understand what it feels like for the child to look different from their parent.
- To have a parent that has knowledge of special dietary, skin, hair, and health care needs.

This list was excerpted from the *Transracial Parenting Resource Manual: Transracial Parenting Project*, page 34 (The North American Council on Adoptable Children, 1998). Reprinted with the permission of the Minnesota Department of Human Services.

Developing a Cultural Plan:
An Adoptive Parent's Perspective

by Leah Dobell

When I became a foster parent in August of 1999, I had no intention of adopting any of the children who would be placed in my care. Little did I know that I would fall madly and irrevocably in love with the jittery, cranky newborn boy of Aboriginal descent who was my first foster child and whom I now call my son.

My son was originally in care by agreement and the plan was for him to return to his birth mom. It soon became clear, however, that his birth mom, who used alcohol and crack cocaine on a daily basis while she was pregnant, was not able to parent him. The care agreement was revoked. By mid-November, he was in continuing custody of the Ministry of Children and Family Development (MCFD). The plan was now for adoption.

By the time my son's file was transferred to a Guardianship and Adoption Social Worker in January 2000, it was becoming clear to me that I wanted to adopt him. My son is Aboriginal and I am not and MCFD's policy is that an Aboriginal child must be placed in an Aboriginal adoptive home. Exceptions to this policy are granted only when all other possibilities have been exhausted and placement in the proposed non-Aboriginal home is the only option seen to be in the child's best interest. All I could do at that time was express my interest in adopting the baby if no Aboriginal homes were found and wait.

Creating Ties

Although things moved relatively quickly, the wait seemed endless. By the spring of 2000, the Social Worker had been in contact with the Social Development Worker from my son's Band and had spoken with a number of extended family members. Nobody had come forward to adopt him; however, an extended family member and his wife had expressed interest in being long-term foster parents. Although only adoptive homes were being considered at that time, the Social Worker and I agreed that it would benefit my son to meet some of his extended family members.

We had an eventful spring and summer! In May, we met extended family members, whom we now consider my son's aunt and uncle. We had several more visits with them and their daughter throughout the summer. I shared with them my wish to adopt the baby, and they were very supportive. They suggested that I contact the Band's Social Development Worker directly.

History of Abuse

In June, I prepared a card and some pictures for my son's birth mom, who had been absent from his life since August 1999. The Social Worker tried, unsuccessfully, to send them through her Financial Aid Worker. In early August, I happened to see my son's birth mom walking on the street and we arranged to have breakfast together. She looked through our photo album and I gave her some pictures to keep. She disclosed the extent of her drug and alcohol use during her pregnancy and expressed a great deal of guilt. I learned that our son's birth father threw her out when he discovered she was pregnant and that she was homeless for most of her pregnancy. I told her of my wish to adopt her son and she, also, was supportive. I expressed my hope that she choose to be part of his life. We went together to see my son's Social Worker. My child's birth mom told the Social Worker that she did not wish her son to be placed with any members of her family and that, "he can stay where he is." I also received word that a family from my son's Band had expressed an interest in adopting him.

Concerns for the Child

By this time, I felt certain that it was in my son's best interest that he be adopted by me; I had concerns about any harm that might be done by moving him.

In early September, I chose to contact the Band Social Worker directly, and to express my concerns, in writing, to my son's Social Worker and her supervisor. Finally, MCFD decided that I was the most suitable adoptive parent; the family who had expressed an interest in adopting him decided to withdraw their application; my son's Band supported me. My sense of relief was indescribable. However, there was much work to be done.

Adoption Application

In order for me to adopt my son, an exception to MCFD's Aboriginal adoption policy was needed. To obtain this exception, an application had to be submitted to the Exceptions Committee. The application process included a written report from the child's Social Worker detailing the attempts that had been made to find an Aboriginal home for the child. The report also discussed the Aboriginal community's participation in the plan to place the child in the proposed non-Aboriginal home.

In addition, the Social Worker outlined my son's history and needs and how my home would meet those needs. Also included was a Cultural Plan. This plan, usually written by the child's Social Worker in consultation with the Aboriginal community and the adoptive parents, describes in detail how my son's cultural identity will be maintained.

The Cultural Plan

I felt strongly that I should write my son's Cultural Plan myself; there were a number of reasons for this. Since I had already established preliminary relationships with my son's birth mom, aunt and uncle and the Band's Social Development Worker, I felt that I might be in a better position for this kind of communication. In fact, I hoped that the process of cultural planning would help to develop these relationships. Nobody could know better than I what would work for me and my family. Finally, I thought that writing the Cultural Plan myself would help demonstrate my commitment to preserving my son's cultural identity. In November 2000, my son and I traveled to his Aboriginal community to meet with the Social

Development Worker. We had a wonderful visit.

I returned home, ready to begin developing my Cultural Plan. My son's Social Worker had provided me with a sample Cultural Plan, which demonstrated the expected format and contents. By January 2001, I had completed a first draft, which I submitted to the Social Development Worker, my son's Social Worker and my Adoption Social Worker for comments and suggestions.

The Cultural Plan described the things that I, my son's extended family members and the Band were willing to do to preserve my son's Aboriginal identity. The plan detailed my intention to seek resources, both within the Aboriginal community and near my home, to educate my family about Aboriginal culture and traditions. I described the relationships I had established with my son's biological family and Aboriginal community members and the efforts I had already made to introduce my son to his Aboriginal culture. I also attempted to portray a sense of who I am and my commitment to my son's well being.

MCFD's goal was to have the application for exception ready in March 2001. By this time, the Band's Chief had written a beautiful letter expressing the Band's support of my adoption. Late in March, I received good news: the exception had been approved, with the condition that a slightly revised copy of the Cultural Plan, signed by me and a representative of the Band, would be submitted by the time the adoption was finalized.

The Home Study

We were now able to proceed with the adoption. I had already completed my home study and attended the required Adoption Education Program. I expect that the adoption will be finalized early in 2002.

Although my adoption has proceeded fairly smoothly, there have been some frustrations along the way. I have found that I need to remind myself that while adopting my son is the top priority in my life, it is one of many issues competing for the attentions of both the Band and MCFD.

I feel incredibly fortunate to have been received with such warmth by my son's birth family and Aboriginal community. I am convinced that these relationships will have many benefits for my son and that our family will be enriched by his Aboriginal culture. It is likely that my wonderful little boy will face many challenges in his life. I am grateful that he will have the love and support of both his adoptive and biological families, as well as his Band, to see him through.

See the following accompanying sample cultural plan.
This article originally appeared in the SNAP newsmagazine, Vol. 17#6, November/December 2001.

SAMPLE CULTURAL PLAN

(provided by Stuart Rennie, Social Worker, and Leah Dobell)

_____demonstrated a respect for and willingness to preserve _____s cultural identity. The following plan for maintaining _____cultural identity has been mutually developed between _____and the _____First Nation.

_____ , Adoptive Parent, agrees to:

Community Contact
-maintain regular contact with the identified community contacts as follows
-visit the_____reserve with _____a minimum of once each year (more likely two or three times each year); _____ will make every effort to schedule these visits around special events on-reserve
-monthly contact with at least one of the community contacts by phone, fax, letter or e-mail-send or deliver photos to Councillor _____ at   least twice yearly
-send or deliver a written progress report to Councillor _____ at least once yearly
-participate with _____in_____cultural events when possible
-allow _____to accompany _____and_____to cultural events which _____is unable to attend
-learn how to prepare and serve some traditional foods; purchase traditional foods and ingredients from_____Band members, when possible
-make every effort to meet with the identified community contacts should they travel to Vancouver; welcome the community contacts in the_____home

Natural Family Contact:
-continue attempts to establish contact with _____; when possible send pictures through _____'s friend
-keep _____'s full name, as chosen by _____ intact as part of his new legal name
-facilitate visits between _____ and _____, _____and _____as follows
-at least monthly phone contact with_____and/or _____
-at least bi-monthly visits with the_____family,_____ at either the_____ home, the home or a mutually agreed-upon location
-remain open to contact with any natural family members and, when appropriate, facilitate such contact

Other:
-enroll _____in_____childcare center when he turns three, provided a space is available and this program meets _____'s needs and the needs of the family at that time
-attend, with _____at least two Aboriginal cultural events in the Lower Mainland each year
-allow _____to accompany _____and _____ to Aboriginal Cultural events in the Lower

Mainland that _____is unable to attend

-enroll _____in at least one Aboriginal program (e.g. dancing, crafts, Salishan Language, etc) each year, when age-appropriate programs are available at times and locations which are feasible.

_____Cultural Worker, VACFaSS, agrees to

-keep _____on the mailing list for the monthly newsletter for caregivers of Aboriginal children

-assist _____, as required, in locating and accessing appropriate cultural programs for in Vancouver.

The_____First Nations Agrees to

-four contact people (Councillor_____ ; Councillor _____, Elder _____,Social Development Worker_____)_____who are willing to work with_____to ensure that 's cultural identity is established and maintained, have already been identified.

- _____will notify _____of any_____cultural events and, when possible, will accompany and _____ to such events

-contact persons will notify _____ when feasible, of planned travel to Vancouver and, if possible, meet with _____ and _____while in Vancouver.

-The Band will keep _____ on the mailing list for the _____ First Nation's Newsletter

-the_____community will welcome _____and his adoptive family on the_____ reserve and at cultural events.

-_____, ____ and __will educate ___and _____regarding traditional teachings and practices of the_____First Nation

-_____and _____will teach _____ how to prepare some traditional foods; they will assist _____ as appropriate, in purchasing traditional foods and ingredients from _____ Band members

-_____ will give _____ information about the history of _____'s natural family, as much as she is able

_____ , the above-named community contacts and the _____ First Nation agree to follow the provisions for confidentiality and discloser of information pursuant to Section (62) of the Adoption Act.

The Cultural Plan will be reviewed by the parties on an annual basis and changes made as required.

Signed (below are spaces for Adoptive Parent, Adoption Social Worker, MCFD Councillor M from _____ First nation and Councillor B from _____ First Nation and Councillor C from _____ First Nation

Prejudice-Sensitive Kids:
How to Help Your Children Bridge Cultural Gaps
by Ann M. Angel

Imagine a world where people aren't victimized because of their religious, ethnic, or cultural backgrounds; a world where children embrace cultural diversity and are equally thrilled to celebrate Cinco de Mayo, Juneteenth Day, Hanukkah, or St. Patrick's Day. A world where kids readily contemplate foreign travel and have globally broad groups of friends.

We can make this kind of world possible for our children by encouraging their awareness and acceptance of other people and other cultures. Although school teachers across the country are working to educate kids about other cultures, parents too must do their part. By opening children up to many cultures through multicultural friendship and experiences, literature, and the media, we can help them recognize stereotypes and racism and bridge cultural gaps that without our help will continue to exist.

Children Learn What They Live

"Kids act out what they experience in their homes," says Steven Baruch, human resource curriculum developer for the Milwaukee Public School system. "If parents live prejudice-free lives, their children will follow suit." A child who sees Mom and Dad with friends of different races will grow up expecting to have transracial friendships; a child who sees men and women in non-traditional roles will grow up expecting to live this way also.

Setting an appropriate example for our children, though, may mean making an effort to stretch our own knowledge and acceptance of other cultures. People sometimes fear the unknown and hesitate to join groups whose members appear different from themselves. "The less people know about another group, the more suspicious of that group and the more intimidated by it they are," explains Edith Adekunle-Wilson, a family living educator with the University of Wisconsin Cooperative Extension. "To be in a better position to be accepting, parents need to seek out the facts. Fantasies and misinformation make it easy to fear, be prejudiced against, or suspicious of others."

Experts agree that the worst thing parents can do is give kids the idea that differences are to be feared. If parents don't step beyond their suspicions and fears, kids won't either. Adekunle-Wilson advises "broadening the parents' and family's facts about and exposure to different racial groups." By reading about other cultures, stepping into multicultural experiences, and cultivating multicultural friendships, parents can overcome their own fears and be better prepared to help their children overcome theirs.

Multicultural Experiences

Parents tend to spend considerable time and energy entertaining their kids. For those who are serious about encouraging multicultural understanding, it would take little effort to ensure that at least some entertainment is multicultural. Remember, though, that the experiences should extend across economic as well as multicultural boundaries. We need to help our kids meet people of all ethnic and racial backgrounds and from all economic groups.

"Don't treat multicultural experiences as exotic though," Baruch warms. "All cultures share with each other, and the experience should be one of sharing." For example, children taken to a performance of African-American folk dancers or Native American storytellers should be encouraged simply to enjoy the performance. As a way to help children see that many cultures share similar values though their traditions vary, parents might want to discuss similarities and differences in the entertainment.

World festivals, organized by many cities to enhance multicultural understanding within their communities, provide a unique multicultural experience. Because these often consist of multicultural exhibits and entertainment, visitors can enjoy the food, arts, traditions, and clothing of several ethnic groups at once—in a celebrative atmosphere. "It's like being invited into each group's world," Adekunte-Wilson says. She stresses, though, that it is important to go beyond celebrations and learn the facts about ethnic contributions to local communities.

For those who live in small towns, multicultural experiences may be harder to find. Planning a family vacation to a larger city to coincide with one of these festivals might be a good way to take advantage of opportunities not available locally. Travelling to find celebrations might not be necessary though. Over the past few years, cultural diversity has become a primary educational focus at the nation's colleges and universities. If you live near a college, call for a schedule of multicultural events.

If multicultural experiences are not available in your community and a vacation is not an option, you might want to organize your own ethnic celebration, All you need is a group of willing friends, an ethnic cookbook, and a little information about the culture you wish to celebrate. Each friend or family can research and be responsible for one aspect of the celebration. For example, one family could organize an ethnic fashion show another could share folk tales and songs, and another might teach new customs to the group. Have each family or friend bring an ethnic dish to share.

Multicultural Friendships
Our churches, schools, and communities provide opportunities to cultivate multicultural friendships. My husband and I have developed culturally diverse friendships through adoption support groups, and I have developed others through my teaching, speaking, and writing. A modern dance class gave my daughter Stephanie, an African-American, an opportunity to expand her friendships. She met other African-American children and Korean-American children and learned a lot about both cultures. Because her dance teacher placed importance on the roots and traditions of American music, Stephanie also discovered that blues and jazz were both developed by African-Americans in new Orleans and Harlem. My sons, Joseph, a Mexican-Indian, and Nick, of Slavic descent, have met kids of other nationalities and races through a culturally diverse, city-wide baseball league.

Finding community members of Native American, African-American, Hispanic, Hmong, or even East Indian descent is usually easy whether you live in a small town or big city. By attending community events and greeting others around you, you open yourself to friendship opportunities.

Beware of Subtle Stereotypes
Although experiencing new cultures increases our sensitivity to them, we still need to be aware of the subtle ways that stereotypes are perpetuated. Even the most well-intentioned of us can slip into cultural stereotyping. Baruch points out the many terms that have crept into our language as examples of how we fall into stereotyping without thinking. The word gypped perpetuates the notion that an entire group of people—gypsies—are cheats. Paddy wagon, derived from the Irish name Paddy, perpetuates the image of the Irish as lawless.

Stereotypes are perpetuated in other ways, too. The Crayola crayon company's designation of one colour as "flesh" feeds into racial stereotyping. (These crayons, sold in the 64 count boxes, were replaced last year with crayons in five flesh tones.) The TV and movie industries are also guilty of stereotyping.

According to Baruch, "Kids see a lot of stereotypes on television and in movies. We can't just plop them down and expect them to develop a global perspective based on the characters they observe." Television can show our kids other cultures though, so we shouldn't just turn the television off. If we pay attention to what our children are watching, we can help them process what they see. Baruch suggests talking to our children as things come up. Pointing out stereotyping helps them become more sensitive to subtle racism.

"White privilege," a term recently coined by Peggy McIntosh, an associate director of the Wellesley College Center of Research on Women, is another subtle form of racism that we can teach our children to recognize. According to McIntosh, white privilege is "an invisible package of unearned assets that Caucasian members of America's society can count on cashing in each day but about which they remain oblivious." These provisions, a "weightless knapsack of special maps, passports, codebooks, visas, clothes, tools, and blank checks," include the opportunity to purchase or rent a home in a location of choice, to be in the company of Caucasians most of the time, and to see Caucasians widely represented on television or the front page of the newspaper. White privilege also includes the opportunity to go out alone most of the time assured of not being harassed because of being different. It is the chance to use credit cards or checks without being questioned about financial responsibility.

When children pick up attitudes or ideas about ethnic groups that are unacceptable to us, Adekunle-Wilson says it is important to gently but firmly correct them. "Personalize examples, "she says. "Bring it home to them by saying, 'If this were you or your brother, how would you feel?" Adekunle-Wilson also says that when a child is a victim of racism or hate, we should point out that the act of hate wasn't nice, then help the child understand what the appropriate way to act should have been. "We can always encourage our children to think about what is the nice thing to do."

Let Your Voice Be Heard
Simply calling our children's attention to stereotyping and racism is not enough. Bigotry comes from many sources, and when we as parents see it in our surroundings, we need to speak up. Our silence, says Adekunle-Wilson, "is an affirmation of others' intolerance. Break the silent agreement."

Speaking up doesn't mean attacking. We can easily tell someone, "I don't think that's funny," in response to an ethnic joke. Or we can ask an intolerant or insensitive speaker, "Do you have any idea how awful what you said sounds?"

A few years ago, a neighbour used the term "nigger" in my kitchen. When I asked her not to talk like that in my house, she responded that my children were bound to hear that kind of language elsewhere. "Yes," I said, "But they have a right to be protected from it in their own home."

I remember this incident because it was the first time I spoke out like this. It was not comfortable, but I felt good after saying what needed to be said. The experience taught me that if I speak out I might be able to defend my children's right to grow up without prejudice. The neighbour blushed, but she didn't storm out of the house. In fact, she has visited my house since and has never used that term around me again. I hope that she took the experience further though. I hope it taught her to think twice before stereotyping all people.

We need to welcome the challenge of living a culturally diverse lifestyle and keep in mind that people who grow to adulthood unable or unwilling to accept and embrace differences will be handicapped in our future.

This article originally appeared in OURS magazine, May-June 1994, pp.20-22. Reprinted by permission of OURS magazine, © 1994 Adoptive Families of America, Highway 100 North, Minneapolis, MN 55422

Capabilities of Persons who Parent Cross-Racially/Culturally

To meet the identity needs of children who live with a family of a race or culture other than their own, it is desirable that persons who parent these children possess the following capabilities:

1. An understanding of their own sense of personal history and how that helped form their values and attitudes about racial, cultural and religious similarities and differences.

2. An understanding of racism and whose life experiences have given them an understanding of how racism works and how to minimize its effects.

3. Life experiences and personal history which have given them the capacity or ability to parent cross-racially/culturally.

4. Commitment to and capability of demonstrating empathy with the child's family of origin regardless of the socioeconomic and lifestyle differences between them and the child's family.

5. Capacity and commitment to provide the child with positive racial and cultural experiences and information and knowledge of their race and culture.

6. Capability of preparing the child for active participation in or return to the

child's racial and cultural community.

7. Adequate support of those significant to them in their decision to parent cross-racially culturally.

8. Residence in a community that provides the child with same race adult and peer role models and relationships on an ongoing basis.

9. Tolerance and ability to deal appropriately with the questions, ambiguity or disapproval which arise when people assume that the child is the applicant's birth child.

10. Willingness to incorporate participation in cross-racial/cultural activities into their lifestyle and participate in race/cultural awareness training

11. Acknowledgment that interracial/intercultural parenting makes their family an interracial/intercultural family which will have an impact on all family members and that a decision to adopt interracially will make the family interracial forever.

12. Acknowledgment and preparedness to deal positively and effectively with the fact that as an interracial family they will experience discrimination similar to other minority families.

13. The skills, the capacity, interest, and commitment to learn parenting skills necessary to parent children to understand and accept their race and racial identity and to work to change the feelings of children who deny their racial identity.

14. Skills, the capacity, and interest to learn the skills to meet the child's special dietary, skin, hair, and health care needs.

15. Appreciation of the child's uniqueness, and at the same time, help the child have a sense of belonging and full family membership.

This list was excerpted from the *Transracial Parenting Resource Manual: Transracial Parenting Project*, page 34 (The North American Council on Adoptable Children, 1998). Reprinted with the permission of the Minnesota Department of Human Services.

To Bring Back Yesterday:
The Story of First Nations' Adoptions
by Susan MacRae

When SNAP first asked me to write an article on First Nations adoptions, I hesitated. How can I write truly on what still is a complex and emotionally painful issue? And how can I, as a non-native person writing to a generally non-native audience, explain in an article the whole political, social, and emotional ramifications of First Nations' adoptions? In other words, how could I touch the pain, and the healing, that Fara sings about in *"To Bring Back Yesterday"* (see inset), that is happening in First Nations' communities, even as I write this article.

So, I decided to start with my own history: namely, the attitudes towards native people that I grew up with in Alberta. One of my early memories is of accidentally walking in on a native family inside their teepee at the Calgary Stampede. I was about six when I walked over to the teepee, pulled back the flap and startled the family just about to eat dinner. Luckily, they didn't yell at me to get out. Embarrassed, I pulled down the flap, and went back to my own family. I remember how it smelled inside the teepee, of the campfire for the dinner, the sunlight coming through the canvas walls, and of another smell that I now recognize to be that of sweet-grass. I also remember that the reason I opened the flap in the first place was because I was told that there wouldn't be anyone inside the teepee, that they were just "part of the show" at the Calgary Stampede. Little did I know that I would interrupt a family during dinner in their home, the same kind of home that was and continues to be part of Plains Indian culture.

My French Canadian grandfather owned a mill on Blackwater Road in Prince George. Around the same time as my Calgary Stampede incident, a native family moved onto the Crown land near the mill into a little shack. My grandfather used to have long conversations with the six-year-old son of the family. According to my grandfather, they would talk quite a bit as the little boy played with a Tonka truck in the dirt and smoked a cigarette. Luckily, I don't remember my grandfather being judgmental of the little boy, or of the family in the shack; in fact, aside from the fact that the boy was only six, my grandfather seemed to have spoken to the boy as if they were having a man-to-little-man conversation. I remember being jealous of the little boy because first, he was "allowed to smoke cigarettes" (something definitely only in the adult realm of allowable activities), and second, that my grandfather treated him as an equal to an adult, even though the boy was my same age. Looking back on my grandfather's actions, I see how complex the interaction was. Having grown up poor himself in a shack with a family of 14 children in Quebec, possibly my grandfather had to have become a "little man" like the little native boy at the same age.

Still, however, the native family on the mill property was never asked to dinner at my grandparents' house in town, and I never did meet the cigarette-smoking little boy. Later, as I grew up in Edmonton, the segregation between my family and aboriginal families continued. We didn't live in the same neighbourhoods, and the reserves were either on outskirts of the city, or in smaller towns. My parents did not have any native friends in my early childhood, and although never spoken out loud, associating with native people was just "not done" among my parents' friends. Every year, at the Edmonton Exhibition, when all the teenagers of Edmonton converged on the fairgrounds, there was always some fight or another between native teens and non-native teens. In fact, the women's washroom at the Ex was a deadly place to hang out, since there was always sure to be a conflict between the native girls and the mostly white girls who I grew up with. Young native girls were always seen as "easy," (generally because young native mothers would keep their children and so be seen on the street, whereas a white girl would be expected to choose an adoption plan for her child—or, even more secretly, have an abortion.) And nobody went down 97th Street in downtown Edmonton after dark because of all the "drunken Indians."

For the past five years, I have been involved in a committed relationship with my partner Molly. Molly is Cree/Sarcee, also from Edmonton. In the course of our relationship, I have had to rethink the attitudes I learned about First Nations' people while growing up. Sometimes it has been difficult to acknowledge my own ignorance about native people, as well as to acknowledge that I have indeed grown up with the insidious belief that the white, middle-class, Christian-based culture is the superior culture, and how everyone *should* be. I have also learned a great deal of history concerning residential schools, natives not being allowed to vote until 1960, land claims issues, the Indian Act and reserve system, as well as traditional spiritual beliefs, such as the medicine wheel and the four directions. And it struck me how I could grow up living on land that had been walked on for thousands of years by a nation of people—in fact, living right next door to the same nation of people—and yet, still be so woefully ignorant about them.

I speak about my own story with my partner Molly and the history of my own attitudes because, as special needs adoptive parents of First Nations children, you will go through much of the same re-learning process I am going through. You will have to look at the attitudes you grew up with and question why you were taught that way. You will learn how the history of the First Nations has affected the life of your child. And, as a transracial adoptive parent, both you and your child will continue to face many of the ignorant beliefs and attitudes that I grew up with in Alberta, from both non-native and native people. However, if you do choose to navigate through some very complex questions, to keep an open mind, and to face the difficulties of raising a special needs child, and specifically, a First Nations child, you will have the opportunity to become, (in the words of Sharon Jinkerson, an adult First Nations adoptee,) "bigger than yourself." You will have the opportunity to become an instrument of healing for your child, for the First Nations community, and for the non-native community as well. Or, in the words of Fara's song, you can help *rebuild the bridge between the old ways and the new* for your child. And also, possibly, for yourself.

Some History

The book *Stolen from Our Embrace: The Abduction of First Nations Children and the Restoration of Aboriginal Communities* (Douglas & McIntyre 1997), written by Suzanne Fournier and Ernie Crey, tells the history of residential schools, as well as the history of the foster care and adoptive systems' policies and practice with regards to aboriginal children. The book grew out of the life story of Ernie Crey, one time President of the United Native Nations, First Nations advocate, and member of the Slo:lo Nation, or People of the River. One of eight children of a residential school survivor father and a tuberculosis-ridden mother, Ernie was taken away in 1961 after his father died, during what would be later known as the "Sixties Scoop." Ernie was placed in a jail cell at twelve years old, and then later transferred to Brannan Lake Industrial School on Vancouver Island, far away from his family. At the school, he experienced sexual abuse from members of the staff until finally he was transferred to non-native foster homes. Although his mother was still trying to contact Ernie while he was a government ward, the Ministry prevented her letters from reaching him. Ernie experienced further sexual abuse after being transferred to a group home. Finally, in 1969, at the age of twenty, he was released from "government care." His family, however, would never be reunited.

Stolen from Our Embrace details Ernie's story, as well as other survivors of the residential and foster-care systems. It provides a historical overview of the Canadian government's assimilation policies, and the ensuing destruction of native families. It also recounts historical facts not often brought up in Canadian history classes even today: for example, the Department of Indian Affairs admitted by the early 1920's "that fifty per cent of the children who passed through these [residential] schools *did not live* to benefit from the education which they received therein." And what kind of education did they receive "therein"? According to Indian Affairs' own statistics in 1930, 75 per cent of aboriginal students across Canada were stuck below Grade 3. Only three in a hundred ever went past

Grade 6. As Musqueum leader Wendy Grant-John stated in 1991 to the Royal Commission on Aboriginal Peoples: "These were not places of learning: they were nothing but internment camps for children."

The last residential school closed in 1984. However, it has only been in the last ten years that First Nations people have been able to speak out against the physical, emotional and spiritual abuse they suffered at residential schools. Even to this day, many elders cannot bring themselves to speak of the deaths (either by beatings, or by children trying to escape the school) they witnessed. There are still many secrets unspoken; or, the secrets died with the victims in violent deaths, in alcoholism, or of never being able to recover a broken spirit.

The deliberate assault on First Nations people in residential schools created the conditions for the next wave of child abductions from the family unit through the foster care system as sanctioned by Child Welfare. Although they might have survived the residential school, children who returned home to their impoverished reserves to their families after being away for more than ten years often did not know how to bond, or communicate with each other. "By the late 1940s, four or five generations had returned from residential schools as poorly educated, angry, abused strangers who had no experience in parenting" (p 82).

In 1959, only 1 percent of children living in foster care were native. By the late 1960s, however, "30 to 40 percent of all legal wards were aboriginal children." Instead of providing safe drinking water, hospitals, social programs, and sanitation to improve Third World conditions on the Reserves, Ottawa decided to take the aboriginal child out of the community. "The white social worker, following hard on the heels of the missionary, the priest and the Indian agent, was convinced that the only hope for the salvation of the Indian people lay in the removal of their children. Adoptive families were encouraged to treat even a status Indian child as their own, freely erasing his or her birth name and tribe of origin, thus implicitly extinguishing the child's cultural birthright. In the foster care system, where native children typically bounced from home to home, a child's tribal identity usually became lost altogether" (p 84).

Doug's Story

Douglas Nichol is a living example of the effects of intergenerational trauma. Born in Vancouver General in 1963 to a Heltsiuk mother from Bella Bella, Doug was adopted by his adoptive parents Adele and Fred Nichol at the age of 3 months.

"I chose her [Adele]," Doug says. "She went walking by the crib and I reached out to her—almost as if to say 'pick me!'" Adele did, in fact, choose Doug and brought him home to Lynn Valley and an adopted older brother, an adopted older sister, as well as numerous native foster children.

But Doug's problems were far from over. "I was born angry, and full of fear of reaction," Doug says. Born with Heiner's syndrome, Doug was pretty much "allergic to anything and everything." He explains, "I hated being this 'special boy', who could only eat rice and drink soy milk."

By the time he was seven, Doug started drinking alcohol and doing petty crime. Adele brought Doug to a psychiatrist because of the behavioural problems he was having. Doug was playing with the toys in the psychiatrist's office, when the doctor came in the door and suddenly boomed at the young Doug: "If you don't stop doing this stuff you are going to go to jail! You're going to die in jail!". Doug ran completely frightened and crying from the psychiatrist's office into Adele's arms, never to return.

By the time Fred and Adele divorced, Doug was the last of the adopted and foster children at home. He was well into the drug scene of the Downtown Eastside. But, in 1986, while living at the Central City Mission, something happened. Doug received a phone call.

Doug was just sitting down to dinner at the Mission when he was called over to the communal phone. "Is this Douglas Nichol?" The voice asked. "Yes," replied Doug. "This is your Aunty Connie." At first, Doug says that he thought his older brother Bruce was playing a joke on him. But, after a second phone call, he discovered that it was not a joke. That, in fact, his birth family in Bella Bella was trying to make contact with him again.

After the phone call from his Aunty Connie, Doug embarked on the process of rediscovering his birth family and the story of how he came to be adopted. At first, he says, his adopted mother felt threatened by the contacts with his birth family. "There's enough love to go around," Adele told him. Doug recognizes that his adopted mother was fearful that he would just pack up and leave and never have contact with his adopted family again. But Doug reassured his mother that he still cared about her, but he needed to discover who he was, and where he came from.

In the process of rediscovering his birth family, Doug learned about the trauma surrounding his birth, which gave him some clues to his subsequent problems with addiction. His mother was angry and did not want the child she was carrying—neither did his grandmother nor any of the other relatives. Learning the story around his birth and adoption has been an extremely difficult and complex process for Doug; the reunion unveiled many secrets that had been hidden for years, and was painful for everyone, including his adoptive parents. However, Doug has thankfully come to the conclusion that he, as a child, was not to blame for his parents' trauma, or his grandparents' trauma. If it were not for the abuse that took place at the residential schools, he feels he would have not inherited his mother's, his father's, and his grandparent's anger, even while in his mother's womb. Nor was he to blame for his adoptive parents' attitudes towards native culture. Although both Doug's families, birth and adoptive, have their differences, each, in their own way, is slowly willing to face the pain of the past in order for Doug to become the man he was meant to be.

Doug now has four years clean and sober with Narcotics Anonymous. He facilitates a healing circle for other First Nations' people to recover from addictions at Four Quarters Institute in Vancouver, and participates in traditional sweat lodge ceremonies. He is an excellent artist and carver, and prays and dances every year in Sundance. In a recent conversation with the same grandmother who didn't want him at birth, Doug's grandmother asked "what do you do in those sweats?"

"I pray. I pray for Mother Earth, Father Sky, all my relations," Doug replied. "I pray for you, too." "Oh, that's good," his grandmother said. "You keep on doing that."

Sharon's Story
Sharon Jinkerson is an advocate for First Nations adoptees. Born in 1957 to Saulteaux/Plains Ojibway (Anishanabe) parents who moved to northern BC to work on the Alaska Highway, Sharon was apprehended from her birth mother at the age of six months by Social Services and put into 17 different foster homes before she was placed with the Jinkersons.

Sharon describes the Jinkersons as "the typical middle-class white family," and Sharon herself as a child could pass for a white girl as she has green eyes and fairish skin. It wasn't until 1964, however, that Sharon was legally adopted by the Jinkersons because, despite not having any legal support or any other form of advocacy, Sharon's birth mother refused to sign the adoption papers. Her mother had not wanted to give her up, totally unbeknownst to the seven-year old Sharon.

The Jinkersons loved their adopted daughter, and raised her the only way they knew how: as a typical white middle class girl of the sixties, along with their three birth children. During Sharon's childhood, they tried to make an effort at acknowledging her "Indian-ness," again, in the only way they knew how: by taking her to the museums to look at artifacts. However, although the Jinkersons did make an effort to acknowledge her distant past, they did not inform her about her recent past. So, instead of having a positive feeling whenever she saw the masks and artwork in the museum, Sharon says that she had a terribly adverse reaction, and would want to leave the museum right away. "I would get a lump in my throat and want to start crying. I now realize that I was grieving for my lost family," she says.

Like Doug, the opportunity to heal her grief came for Sharon when she finally met her maternal grandmother, Rebecca. Sharon had already begun her process of trying to peel back the layers of secrecy surrounding her past by returning to find her birth family. By that time, to her devastation, Sharon had assimilated many of the racist beliefs about native people from her adoptive family and non-native society. She was told that returning to see her family would be devastating, that her birth family would be full of hate for her and violent, but to her surprise, they welcomed her. Yes, the native community to which she had returned was wounded; however, they still accepted her. And the greatest form of acceptance came from her grandmother, Rebecca.

Rebecca asked to see Sharon's childhood pictures. Although Sharon was reluctant to show her grandmother her past, they did sit down together and go through the photos. They looked at pictures of Sharon as a child dressed up for birthday parties, and at pictures of Sharon's three siblings and adoptive parents. Upon looking at all of these photos, Rebecca pronounced, with no bitterness whatsoever, "you were so loved", and that her adoptive parents had been "honourable people" for taking care of her so well.

In that moment, Rebecca healed the split in Sharon's life between her allegiance to her adoptive family and her deep need to reconnect with her birth family. For Rebecca, love for her grandchild was not an either/or option; it could be both. Despite the pain and mistakes of both of their pasts, Sharon's truth could be accepted by her grandmother. In doing so, Sharon and her grandmother became "bigger than themselves", and like Fara's song, built *a bridge between the old way and the new* to each other. Sharon could finally participate in the rituals that she grieved for at the museums of her childhood.

Sharon continues to this day on the healing journey her grandmother Rebecca set out for her. With the birth of Sharon's son, Solomon, Sharon recovered memories of her own traumatic abduction at the age of six months by social workers from her birth family. She wrote down her memories in a powerfully written piece called "The Dream". She also learned with the birth of her son that her birth mother had not been neglectful when she was a baby; but, rather, that her own son had a hereditary skin disease that Sharon had most likely had as a baby, and that had nothing to do with the quality of her mother's care (despite the reports of Child Welfare.)

Sharon is also writing a children's book called "Aunty Sharon's Visit" that tells the story of a First Nations' adoptee reunion with her birth family, and of an 11 year old niece who comes to know and love her Aunty Sharon. She has also produced a documentary on Aboriginal Adoptions entitled "Inside the Masks"— a poignant referral to the museum masks of her childhood—that she hopes to broadcast on the newly created Aboriginal People's Television Network. And she continues to advocate for First Nations adoptees.

Although Sharon has done a tremendous amount of work to uncover her past and break the cycle of abuse, she knows she is still in the process of healing. Her birth mother died last fall, never having recovered from the loss of her children. And her adoptive father died last spring, never having forgiven or wanting to build a bridge with Sharon's birth family. Sharon's, and her own son Solomon's, healing will continue to take time; however, she has been given the gift of hope by her grandmother Rebecca speaking through the masks of her ancestors to the future generations.

What Adoptive Parents Can Do

Although British Columbia's new *Adoption Act* of 1996 introduced the mandate to place native children in foster care with native adoptive families, and child welfare authority for aboriginal children is starting to be handed over to band office jurisdiction, there are still many non-native families raising native children. And many issues continue to segregate native and non-native people. Despite the obstacles, however, what message of hope can special needs adoptive parents bring to their First Nations' children, and hence, to future generations?

Both Sharon and Doug advocate bringing your child to elders in the aboriginal community. Contact places such as the local Native Friendship Centre, or Vancouver's Four Quarters Institute, where you can be put into contact with other people who follow traditional spiritual beliefs and are in the process of healing.

Also, become open to the possibility of contact with your child's birth parents, if possible. Try to keep the doors open; even if it is not possible now for a healthy interaction between your child and their birth parents, let the child know it could be possible in the future. Or, if the parent is not alive, try to get in contact with members of the parent's extended family. In First Nations culture, it is the community that raises the child, not just the parents. Become willing to open up to a new community.

Advocate for resources for parents of First Nations special needs children. In spite of the provisions of the new *Adoption Act*, Sharon Jinkerson suggests that the provincial government has done little to assist First Nations communities with the new responsibilities, or to create resources for non-native families who raise First Nations children. She suggests a talking circle between the First Nations community and non-native, special needs adoptive parents. In a talking circle, discussion on a subject is lateral, without hierarchical structures, and everybody's opinion is respected. Everybody belongs in a talking circle as well: creating a sense of belonging, and loving your adopted child for who they are, will be the most important things for you to provide your First Nations child.

Finally, the most important task for you as non-native adoptive parent will be looking at yourself and your own attitudes. Become aware of how you were raised to treat or view native people. Look at how our media, our neighbours, and our government treats First Nations politically and socially. Learn about the history of First Nations and adoption by reading books such as *Stolen from Our Embrace*. Bring your child to First Nations events. Find an advocate for your child, whether a relation or not, who can help your child to participate in traditional ceremonies so that they know who they are and where they come from, so they can be proud of their heritage.

Be aware that, although you may love your child, they will never be the "same" as you; they will always be different. Acknowledge and honour both the joy and the pain of your child. In so doing, you can help heal a child, a family, and a nation. But most importantly, you can come to know the power of the Creator in all our lives, and so, come to heal yourself.

Works Cited

"To Bring Back Yesterday", Lyrics & Music by Fara Palmer, Chuck Brickley and Peter Kilgour, Published by Farasongs (SOCAN) and Astral Blue Music (SOCAN) , from the album Pretty Brown, New Hayden Music Corp, 1999.

Suzanne Fournier and Ernie Crey, *Stolen from Our Embrace: The Abduction of First Nations Children and the Restoration of Aboriginal Communities*, Douglas & MacIntyre, Vancouver/Toronto, 1997.

TO BRING BACK YESTERDAY

My mama told me years ago when she was just a girl
About the way that she was raised in residential school
The first thing that happened was they shaved off all her hair
And burned it with her clothes

She told me she was not allowed to speak her native tongue
And I believed they wanted her because she was so young
They said it was their duty to save the little heathen
All in the name of heaven

Who are they to tell us how to live
Who would I be if we hadn't burned the bridge
Between the old ways and the new
There's nothing I can do to bring back yesterday

The song "To Bring Back Yesterday," written by Cree singer/songwriter Fara, speaks of the unspoken cultural war against First Nations people in Canada for the past 100 years, and the resulting intergenerational trauma from residential schools. Fara's song is dedicated to her mother, a survivor of the residential school system. Her mother becomes a warrior, by daring to survive and to continue telling stories about creation that were banned to her mother as a child in residential school. "To Bring Back Yesterday" is a very moving and powerful prayer of healing for the First Nations' community.

LIFE NOT EXISTENCE

My soul walks in the cold feelings of loneliness.
Lying on broken glass with a needle in my arm and a full moon in my eye.
A young boy sneaking outside to climb a tree and feeling the beauty of mother earth and father sky, dreaming of being an artist.
Quivering and shakes, vomit on the floor, and blood on my arm, cold broken heart and death in my eye.
The sun comes up and he goes out to play.
No worries, no pain, God is good, and I will soon go home to eat.
It is too bright and I want it all to fade away, nothing is good anymore.
Falling down and seeing my inner child brings a smile.
Cold sweat forms on my forehead and I'm scared.
I cry for help and God gives me life.
I have found my Creator.
The giver of life is good to me, and now I can see life and not just existence.

—poem by Doug Nichol, adult adoptee

This article originally appeared in the SNAP newsletter, Vol. 15 #4, Winter 2000. © 2000 Society of Special Needs Adoptive Parents

Some Thoughts on Cross-Cultural Adoption:
An Adopted Person's Perspective
by Bruce Leslie

On July 30, 1953, I was born at the regional hospital in Turtleford, Saskatchewan about 70 km north west of North Battleford. I was taken into the care of the Saskatchewan Department of Social Services at birth and adopted at approximately four months of age.

In July 1984, I received an unsigned handwritten letter from my birth mother through a post-adoption social worker in the Department of Social Services in Regina. The text of this letter contained confirmation of what I had suspected since my early teens. I had "some Indian blood from [my] grandfather's side," my birth mother wrote. She identified herself to the social worker of the day as being French.

I was the oldest child in my adoptive family. My middle sister was an adopted Cree, born in Saskatoon. My adoptive step-grandfather was an off-reserve Cree speaker. My adoptive mother and father, who eventually had a natural daughter, were Euro-Canadian and working poor, but good people. I might not have had all the material trappings of the aspiring middle class families in our post-war neighbourhood, but I was raised with kindness and caring.

In my judgement, children in care of the state or adopted may enjoy a more comfortable material life, but do not do so well in their interior life. For me, the emotional consequence of being raised as a white child but having brown skin is that I have never felt as though I fit in. I do not belong to the Native community, nor do I fit into the dominant culture.

In addition to the other by-products of colonialism, the cycle of child welfare has helped to perpetuate the legacy of dysfunction in Aboriginal families and communities. Now the children of children are being taken into the care of the state.

The reality each of you will encounter is that the adoption of an Aboriginal child today into a non-Aboriginal home in BC, carries with it the burden of 500 years of state sanctioned cultural destruction. You will also come to observe, as you help your Aboriginal child maintain connection to his or her Indigenous heritage, that we are not a dead or dying culture. You will discover that Indigenous peoples are alive and well, as we were for tens of thousands of years prior to the arrival of the first Europeans. So today I challenge you to broaden your awareness about First Nations and Metis history in Canada as you embark on your journey with the Aboriginal child you have welcomed into your home and your lives.

I did not have the benefit of knowing who my people were. However today, because of that letter, at least I can think of myself as a Cree/Metis person. Until I can reconnect with my birth relatives, I will never know the strength of my Indigenous heritage. No Aboriginal child should have to live their life trying to be a white person; trying to be something they are not. Nor should they be unable to tell others where they are from and who their ancestors were. First Nations and Metis children deserve to grow up seeing their ancestry as a thing of beauty and strength, and a lifelong source of teachings and traditions.

As the adoptive parents of an Aboriginal child you must help your daughter or son to know who they are and where they came from. You must think about the distant future, when you are no longer here. One day they too will take their last breath on this mother earth. When that time comes, it will be impossible for them to take any of the earthly goods they have inherited from you. They will have to leave behind all the material trappings of their modern urban life, and take only what they have learned from you. Teach them to know their ancestors and help them re-connect with respected Elders from their cultural community.

This article originally appeared in the SNAP newsletter, Vol. 15 #4, Winter 2000. © 2000 Society of Special Needs Adoptive Parents

single parent adoption

PEOPLE THINK IT IS VERY
DIFFICULT TO BE A SINGLE
PARENT. IT IS AND IT ISN'T. THE
SINGLE ADOPTIVE PARENT HAS
HAS MADE A CHOICE TO RAISE
A CHILD ALONE, AND IF THE
DECISION IS WELL THOUGHT
OUT, THE EXPECTATION AND
REALITY ARE NOT TOO
DISPARATE.

    – Andrea, adoptive
    parent

.

Going It Alone

by Katherin Jones

Being a parent is not easy. Doing it on your own, as a single parent, presents additional challenges. You are the anchor, you are everything: the sole breadwinner, caregiver, housekeeper, cook, chauffeur, cuddler and tear-dryer. There is no-one else there to turn to, to help make decisions or to take over when you're exhausted and ready to drop. You are it!

I adopted my son, David, as a single parent. Mine was a typical pre-adoption scenario, miscarriages, infertility, a long adoption search, and at long last, joy of joys, David.

An increasing number of people, mainly women at this point, are choosing to adopt as single parents. For most of us, it is the best moment of our lives. But it ain't easy. There are many days of joy, and many moments of frustration.

Through planning and networking before you adopt, you can make it easier. The best first step you can take is to join an adoption support group. The adoption process can be a rough ride, and you need all the help you can get. Your family and friends may not understand your strong desire for a child, and may not provide the support you need. You have to give people time to get used to the idea, while you persevere. A support group will give you the encouragement of people who have already adopted, or like you, are just beginning.

Building a strong support system, involving family, friends and support groups, makes raising a child on your own easier and more enjoyable.

It's also important to pick the right social worker to do your Home Study. Find someone who is supportive and you feel comfortable with.

Financial security is a major concern for most families. Double that for a single parent family. Many couples and singles borrow money from their families and/or the bank to finance the adoption. Many re-mortgage their home to cover adoption costs. Find out if daycare subsidies are available in your municipality. Prepare a financial plan. (A good guide is *"Personal Finance for the Single Parent"* by Marilyn J. Nichols, page 16 in *The Handbook for Single Adoptive Parents*).

Make a will. A lot of these steps can at least be started before you adopt.

Adoption is complex. Parenting is complicated. Being a single parent is intense, wonderful and fulfilling.

From *Family Helper*, www.familyhelper.net. © 2003 Robin Hilborn. Reprinted with permission.

Being a Single Mom:
An Adoptive Parent's Perspective
by Leah Dobell

I never planned to be the single adoptive parent of a little boy with special needs. Like most girls and young women, I imagined that I would meet "Mr. Right", get married and have birth children. I especially wanted a little girl, and, of course, she would be perfect. Everyone knows that our lives often don't turn out the way we expect they will. In my case, I have no doubt that things turned out exactly the way they were meant to be.

I first met my son, Floyd, at the hospital where he was born. He was two weeks old and was in care of the Ministry for Children and Family Development (MCFD) because he had been exposed antenatally to alcohol, crack cocaine and marijuana. I was to be his foster Mom, and visited him in hospital for two days so that I could get to know him before I took him home. For me, it was love at first sight. Because Floyd had only two visits with his birth Mom, he soon felt very much like my baby. We bonded quickly, strongly and mutually.

As my relationship with Floyd blossomed and strengthened, I became convinced that we belonged together. However, because Floyd is an Aboriginal child, MCFD was searching for a First Nations adoptive home for him. I was told that as a non-Aboriginal person, my chances of adopting Floyd were slim. MCFD's policy in such circumstances is to consider non-Aboriginal adoptive homes only when there are no suitable Aboriginal homes available. Fortunately, with the support of my family and friends, as well as Floyd's birth family and Aboriginal community, MCFD was persuaded that it was in Floyd's best interest to be adopted by me. In January, 2002, when Floyd was two years and five months old, the adoption was finalized. My psychological shift was much greater than I had anticipated. It was as though my role as Floyd's Mom was suddenly legitimized, and somehow there was a new and greater depth in our relationship.

Being Floyd's Mom is more amazing than I could ever have imagined. He brings me such joy every day. Although there are times when I miss having a partner and co-parent, I've discovered some real advantages to single parenting. For example, so many couples seem to have conflict over decisions related to their children. I can, and very frequently do, consult friends, family members and professionals about issues related to parenting and Floyd's special needs. However, I really like the fact that all final decisions are made by me. Although bearing the full responsibility for child-rearing, earning money and managing a household can be stressful, there is something quite rewarding about being self-sufficient. Also, I don't have to deal with disappointment over unmet expectations of a partner's participation in parenting and other joint responsibilities. Knowing, for example, that when I want a break from parenting I need to arrange child care, somehow seems to make life simple. In a way, there is something really wonderful about being Floyd's only parent, and part of me is glad I don't have to share him with anyone.

Despite the joys of single parenting, I do encounter challenges, some of which are compounded by Floyd's special needs. One of my greatest concerns is balancing work, which is necessary to meet our financial needs, with time together. I am fortunate, as a Registered Nurse, that I earn a solid income and there is currently lots of work available. However, being the single parent of a special needs child significantly decreases my flexibility. For example, because of Floyd's special needs, I am very particular about child care. The teenager down the street, for instance, may not be an acceptable option. I am lucky to have Floyd in an excellent daycare program, where the teachers are trained to work with special needs. I also have a wonderful adult caregiver who comes to my home. However, quality child care is expensive. My hours of work must fit the times that I have child care available, since there is no other parent to drop Floyd off or pick him up. Also, as a single Mom, I need a job which provides full benefits and an employer who will allow me to use my sick time if Floyd is ill.

A related consideration is ensuring that Floyd will continue to be provided for in the event of my death or disability. This seems particularly important as Floyd's only parent. Also, my experience as a foster parent has made me very determined that my child will never be "in care." As soon as my adoption was final, I had both a representation agreement and a will prepared, and purchased a life insurance policy. The representation agreement allows my brother to take over management of my affairs, including finances and guardianship of Floyd, in the event that I become mentally incapacitated. The possibility of becoming disabled is an additional reason for choosing a job which provides benefits, particularly sick time and disability insurance. Choosing guardians for a child with special needs is a particularly daunting task. Floyd has been diagnosed with Partial FAS, and although he is making excellent developmental progress, there is a good chance that he will be a challenging child to parent. He will likely need support of some kind for the rest of his life. I am fortunate to have some family members and friends who have stated their willingness to be Floyd's guardians. However, it is difficult to know whether they fully understand the commitment they are making. Also because of Floyd's special needs, I felt it was important to purchase a large enough life insurance policy that his guardians would be able to comfortably meet his needs, with a reasonable sum remaining when he reaches adulthood. Floyd's disability means that I will likely always need a plan in place to provide for him once I am no longer able to.

As the single Mom of a little boy, I also worry about providing Floyd with male role models and exposure to healthy couple relationships. We are lucky to have friends and family willing to act in both of these roles. I also hope that Floyd will meet suitable male role models at school and through activities. However, children with FAS are often particularly susceptible to abuse. Therefore, I will need to be especially cautious about allowing Floyd to spend unsupervised time with adults and older children whom I don't know and trust.

I am very fortunate to have the ongoing support of my family and friends. It helps that my family has experience with both adoption and single parenting. When I made the initial decision to try and adopt Floyd, my parents were supportive, but concerned about how I would cope if MCFD decided that I couldn't adopt him. They also had some concerns about how I would manage financially. Since I was already caring for Floyd and two other children with special needs, it was clear that I could manage the day to day stresses of single parenting. For a variety of reasons, my family and friends are able to provide only limited practical support. However, their emotional support is invaluable.

I receive my most valuable support from others with similar experiences. I have friendships with a number of other adoptive and foster parents. I attend two parent support groups, one for parents and caregivers of children with FAS, and the other for foster parents of children with difficult behaviours. In addition to emotional support, these groups offer the knowledge and experience of group members. This expertise is also available through organizations such as SNAP and the FAS Support Network. I know that I will have many questions as Floyd grows, and I am thankful that such resources are available.

In addition, I have received essential support from the many professionals involved with Floyd and me. Floyd's development is followed regularly by his pediatrician, physiotherapist, occupational therapist, speech and language pathologist, and daycare teachers. These services were all in place before Floyd was adopted, which has been beneficial in two ways. The continuity of these services has made the transitions from foster care to adoption smooth for both

Floyd and me. Also, because most of these professionals have known us since Floyd's infancy, they have supported us throughout the adoption process. Our Adoption Social Worker and my Resource Social Worker have been additional sources of knowledge and wisdom.

It's still hard to believe, sometimes, that Floyd is really mine. I feel so lucky to be the mother of this wonderful little boy. While single parenting is a challenge at times, the few difficulties are more than offset by the many joys. I know that Floyd and I will face more challenges in our future, and I'm grateful to have the formal and informal support we will need to overcome them.

This article was written specifically for this book. © 2002 Society of Special Needs Adoptive Parents

10 Ways to Rejuvenate Your Energy:
Quick Pick-Me-Ups for When You're Stretched to the Limit
by Deborah C. Joy

It's late on Saturday afternoon, and I need help. Despite my valiant efforts to carve out one-on-one time for each of my children, they still seem to be competing for my attention. Daylight is dwindling, and I am still on page one of my to-do list.

In desperation, I reach for the phone. "Nine-one-one...what is your emergency?" I hear the operator ask. In my daydream, I scream into the phone, "I need help over here. I can't do all of this by myself!"

As a single parent (or as any parent), no doubt you've reached the end of your rope from time to time. (Care to count how often?) To prevent any real 911 phone calls from your household, you need to know how to rejuvenate your energy when your children have stretched you to the limit. Here's my top ten list of ways to do that.

1. According to an informal poll of single parents, the most popular way to rejuvenate energy levels is to **get a baby-sitter** and have time away from the children. Just because we single parents spent a great deal of time, energy, and/ or money adopting our children doesn't mean that we don't also occasionally feel exasperated, exhausted, annoyed, and/or angry with them.

You have to dispel the notion that because your children are adopted, you are not allowed to experience this normal range of emotions that all parents experience. A subtle societal message tells us, "You did it to yourself and you shouldn't complain." This is not accurate. You deserve time away from your children. Single parents are always on call. It is extremely important to have time to yourself. Keep in mind the instructions you get when you fly. You know—when the stewardess says if there is a problem put the oxygen mask on *yourself* first. You cannot help your child if you are "out of gas."

2. **Schedule a fun midweek ritual**—don't save all the fun for the weekend! Choose the most difficult night of the week for you and bring in McDonald's, have a picnic on the floor, or leave your children at their caregiver's for an extra hour while you have a little time to yourself. You may be surprised at how much extra energy even an hour alone can give you.

3. **Keep a secret supply of emergency toys**. Save a few small toys from your Christmas or birthday shopping and use them when your children are especially demanding and you could use a break.

4. **Join a support group** and really talk to other members about the problems you're having. This is my personal favorite. Don't feel that you are the only person having difficulties with your children. However, it's important to be able to share tips as well as traumas. Sometimes really small tips can reduce stress in a family considerably.

For example, a friend of mine returned from Guatemala with her baby daughter, who was unable to sleep through the night. When I suggested she put her nightgown in the crib with the baby, the baby was able to sleep better. This obviously reduced stress for both the mother and the child.

5. **Attempt to carve out a space in your house for adults only**. This may be only a small corner of your bedroom, but you can use this space as your own personal retreat when things are tough.

Having a ten minute time-out for yourself can make the difference between that 911 call and being able to cope with the day. It is important to stock this space with your favorite tapes, a book that you enjoy, candy that you like to eat, etc. If necessary, latch your bedroom door shut so that the children are not in that space or whatever space you designate as yours. Kids need to learn boundaries, and this is a good way to teach them. Remember that you are giving them a wonderful role model that they can use when they become parents.

6. **Find a creative outlet for yourself**, preferably one that does not talk back. This is probably the most neglected aspect of the single parent's energy source, but one that gives tremendous pleasure and a renewed sense of energy.

I know a single mother of four who felt a renewed sense of being able to cope after she had sewn outfits for her four children. She lost a bit of sleep over this endeavor, but her sense of accomplishment and pride in her achievement outweighed by far the few minutes of lost sleep.

7. **Cultivate your family's sense of humor**. Family life can be very stressful, and it is important that you learn to laugh at your mistakes and those of your

children. This will also help the kids put their mistakes into perspective and deal with them in a more positive light.

At dinner one night, my oldest daughter was joking about our progress with some of our shortcomings. The conversation went something like this… "Well let's see, Rachel hasn't thrown a tantrum lately, Adam hasn't bitten anyone at day care, you haven't been screaming at us, and I don't have an F in English anymore."

All families have shortcomings and it is important for children to understand that these shortcomings are a part of being human. Not taking mistakes so seriously can improve your energy level tremendously.

8. **Sleep!** Getting enough sleep is perhaps as important as getting away occasionally. There are many ways to get more sleep, such as napping when your baby or toddler naps. Frequently, when I suggest this to parents, I hear that they then won't be able to finish the laundry, pay bills, dust the furniture, etc. That is true. Perhaps those chores won't be accomplished, but you will feel better about not having accomplished them if you get more rest and the chores will be waiting for you another time.

Another way to get more rest is to have a cut-off time at the end of the evening when you promise yourself that you will not do another chore or attend to another detail of your children's day. Instead, you will go to bed with a book, go to bed watching a television show, or call a friend who is still awake (this may not be one of your single parent friends).

9. **Exercise.** Exercise does give people more energy. Some ambitious parents exercise with their babies or toddlers by putting them in a stroller for a jog or a walk. Other parents accomplish having time alone and exercising by taking their children with them to an exercise program that includes baby-sitting for a nominal fee.

10. **Learn to delegate**. I promise you that you cannot do it all. Hire out as many chores as you can afford to hire out. I remember one mother who told me that laundry was her most hated chore and that following the adoption of her first child, she sat by the washing machine and cried. To cope, she found a college student who was happy to earn a few extra dollars by helping with the extra laundry that having children entails.

Perhaps laundry isn't what you dislike the most; perhaps it's cleaning your house or grocery shopping. There are services available to deal with these chores, and even if you treat yourself once a month to one, you will find it improves your energy a great deal.

This article originally appeared in *Adoptive Families* magazine, July/August 1995. Reprinted with permission from Adoptive Families magazine. For more articles like this one, to subscribe or to sign up for the monthly e-newsletter, visit Adoptive Families online, www.AdoptiveFamilies.com.

gay & lesbian adoption

NO MATTER HOW WE CREATE
OUR FAMILIES, WE USUALLY
START OUT PREPARED FOR THE
FACT THAT AT LEAST ONE
PARENT IN THE COUPLE WILL
HAVE NO GENETIC CONNECTION
TO THE CHILD WE RAISE. WE
HAVE THEREFORE ALREADY
OVERCOME THE BIAS WHICH
PRESUMES THAT PARENTING A
CHILD MEANS HAVING A
BIOLOGICAL RELATIONSHIP.

    – April Martin, Ph.D.

—— Gay & Lesbian Adoptive Parenting ——
by Michael Colberg

Gay and lesbian adoptive parenting has come of age. Although the debate regarding whether homosexuals should be allowed to adopt continues, the truth is that gay and lesbian-parented families have, in many ways, become mainstream. Our families are written about, filmed and studied. More and more agencies are training their staff to work with gay and lesbian pre-adoptive couples. Almost all of the major adoption conferences have included this population and have learned from the experiences shared by homosexual parents. We have come a long way.

When my partner and I adopted thirteen years ago, we were hard-pressed to find an agency or attorney who would work with us. We, in effect, had to advocate for ourselves. We were forced to figure out how to adopt from outside the traditional loop. In doing so, we had an opportunity to learn about the essential nature of adoption. I learned that being adopted is not an event, but an ongoing process-- just like being gay. By the time that we became parents, we understood the lifetime nature of adoption and how important it was for a child to know and honor who they are in the fullest sense of the term—even having a relationship with their birth parent if possible.

As I learned more about adoption, I began to find important similarities between the experiences of adoptees and those of homosexuals. For one thing, neither adoptees nor homosexuals are typically parented by members of their minority group. Homosexuals typically have heterosexual parents, and adoptees' parents are generally not adoptees themselves. This means that neither gays nor adoptees are socialized into their minority status by their parents. They have to figure it out on their own. This is unusual. Another similarity is that neither group has the same civil rights as those enjoyed by the population at large. When it comes to our populations, those that argue for small government ironically seem to be the most intrusive. The state continues to intrude on our families in a number of inappropriate ways. These similarities made me realize that I could use my coming out experiences to help me gain empathy for my daughter's feelings about being adopted.

To prepare for becoming parents, we needed to learn about how adoption impacts an adoptee and all of his parents throughout their lives. We already knew about being gay. In doing so, we naturally came to a place where our understanding was child-centered. We learned first about being adopted and then about what parenting through adoption required.

We, as it turns out, were fortunate. One of the dangers present in becoming mainstream is that we are now being invited to join a placement system that focuses on "getting" a child and often ignores what it means to be a good adoptive parent. This means that the gay and lesbian community runs the risk of succumbing to society's insistence that we make gay- and lesbian-parented adoption a gay rights issue rather than about the children and their needs. If we were looking at things in a child-centered way, we would realize that homosexuals who have an understanding of how their experience parallels their children's experiences are especially well-suited to mentor their children.

We also have to understand that being homosexual is not equally important for all gay men and lesbians. We need to pay attention to other layers of diversity including, but not limited to, race, ethnicity, religion, intelligence, economic situation, emotional maturity of the parents, the family's geographic location, the form of the adoption, the nature of the parent's and of the child's larger community. These layers of diversity will need to be addressed by the gay and lesbian communities in the coming years. We are not a single group, but many groups who may share nothing more than sexual orientation. We should use these differences as a way to collaborate, but, unless they are acknowledged, I fear that they will cause some parents in our community to feel further marginalized and alone.

We also need to learn how to focus on and address whatever layer of diversity is important in our children's lives at any given point in time. Sometimes being adopted is more important than having same-sex parents or being of a different race than parents and sometimes having same-sex parents is the focus. It is not always easy to distinguish what is going on. My daughter came home a year or so ago saying that she hated having gay parents. I asked her why and she said that she hated having to explain the whole thing all of the time. She also said that, even after she explained that she had two dads, kids would ask her which of us was her real dad. By this time crying and in my lap, she told me that she would have to tell them that neither of us were. Her sadness was, at that moment, about being adopted, not about having gay dads. I sat with her and we both felt the sadness of not having a biological connection, and then she got up and went back to her life. This could only happen because I had an awareness of the nature of adoption.

Gay and lesbian adoptive parents need to learn that it is vitally important that they become adoption competent. There is a lot of sadness present both for homosexuals during the coming out process and for adoptees as they grow up. If gay and lesbian parents are not educated about adoption, they may feel that they are doing something wrong when their child becomes appropriately sad and they may have some of their shame issues rekindled. It is only when we understand the true and complex nature of adoption that we can make use of our experience, be with our children as they express their feelings and help them to feel proud of who they are in world—just as their parents do.

This article originally appeared in *Decree*, a publication of the American Adoption Congress, Summer 2001. It is reprinted here with permission of the American Adoption Congress.

Survival Tips for Gay & Lesbian Adoptive Parents

by Gladys Fraser & Sara Graefe

Gay and lesbian adoptive families are out there. While biases against gay and lesbian parents continue to exist, many individuals, organizations and even government systems are becoming more accepting of gay and lesbians building families through adoption. Here in British Columbia, the Adoption Act of 1996 expanded eligibility criteria to allow gay and lesbian couples to openly apply for adoption. The legislation has also made it possible for gay men and lesbians to adopt their partner's child from a previous relationship.

As American psychologist and lesbian mom April Martin points out, as gay and lesbians are becoming more visible in the system, word is getting around that they are good parents. Many social workers who wouldn't have dreamed of placing a child in a gay family ten years ago now do so without hesitation. More agencies are happy to facilitate adoption to openly gay applicants. More pregnant birthmothers are choosing open lesbians and gay men to raise the children they are carrying (*The Lesbian and Gay Parenting Handbook*; New York: Harper Collins, 1993).

Even so, as a gay man or a lesbian, you may continue to brush up against subtle and not-so-subtle homophobia as you make your way through the adoption process. You also face a special set of post-adoption concerns. You're dealing with the challenge of being an adoptive parent (often dealing with special needs), coupled with the added challenge of being a gay or lesbian parent in a predominately straight, at times homophobic, world. Like all gay and lesbian parents, you undoubtedly live with the stress of knowing that some people harbour violently negative feelings about your family. Even those who are not actively hostile towards you may distrust your ability to parent. As you venture out into the world with your partner and your adopted child(ren), you may attract attention and stares from even the most benign strangers, simply because you're different. Many straight adoptive parents have complained about feeling as though they're on display and being judged all the time. Gay and lesbian adoptive parents often experience the same thing, only more intensely. It's important to arm yourself with a set of survival and advocacy skills, and to surround yourself with welcoming, supportive, loving allies—people who embrace you as a family, and really "get it."

Gladys Fraser and her partner Sheila were one of the first lesbian couples to complete an adoption under the current legislation in British Columbia. They adopted an older child in small-town BC. Gladys has put together a list of survival tips for other gay and lesbian adoptive parents, based on her family's experiences:

• Make certain that you are satisfied that the support people in your lives are truly accepting. We had the experience of a physician who we believed was accepting until he made a referral to a child psychiatrist for our daughter. We had made the decision to stay with her previous physician with the idea that this would mean one less disruption/change for her. On first meeting him he was friendly and when he understood that we jointly adopted our daughter his response was generally "Cool" (as in, "that's great!") which led us to believe he was supportive and that we could work with him. It wasn't until over a year later when we needed his assistance with a referral to the psychiatrist that we realized his bias. He started the conversation asking us if we didn't think that she was actually just confused and ashamed of having two Moms. His referral stated "I am making this referral for... As you can see from their names this is a lesbian couple." What did this have to do with our daughter's medical condition? This became the last contact we had with this doctor and our daughter switched to see our family physician.

• Expect that even the social workers who believe you are good candidates for adoption may not consider you for situations where the birth parents or extended family has some involvement. While on the surface the workers may appear accepting, they won't go to bat for you or the child if they think another interested party may be homophobic even if this means the child will stay in the system longer. One social worker told us outright that no parent would choose to place their child with a same sex couple or homosexual individual over a heterosexual—that we could certainly enter the process but don't expect to have much interested response. "Blue slips" (as they are known) provide a response to your unsuitability for a child the Ministry is trying to place. Our homestudy travelled throughout the province actively, and our file contained over 30 blue slips in a 50 week period. Most came back without an explanation, but those that did indicated some concern about extended family being unwilling to consider a same sex couple.

• Really know your help and support people. Don't rely on a Social Worker's recommendation for any individuals who may become part of your care circle (eg. respite homes, counsellors, etc). We had a Social Worker highly recommend a respite home for our daughter. It met many of our basic criteria and upon first meeting we outright asked about their views of same sex couples parenting. The Social Worker actually rolled her eyes at this question and almost excused our behaviour as she was uncomfortable with this questioning. The woman in this respite home clearly explained that their church states that they must accept everyone, and she understands the MCF policy etc. etc. When we actually went for a second visit to this family home, it became apparent that they clearly do not support same sex couples adopting, let alone parenting, period. Had we relied on the Social Worker's recommendation, our family would have been very quickly jeopardized by this couple's intention to "save our child". They fundamentally believed that we were the only problem without ever meeting our child!

• Hang out with gay couples you know who have children. Find out what their experiences have been in your community. As with straight couples who become parents, often your friends without children will drift away. They don't understand that you can't stay out late, or just pick up and go any time. In our situation we had to be extremely careful on the choice of babysitter due to our daughter's special needs and this meant we were even more limited. Some people can't relate, and even in the gay world there is an element of the community that doesn't support the idea of gays and lesbians raising children. Even those in the community who are supportive may be unable to relate if they haven't chosen to parent themselves. On top of this, some of your peers may have their own issues with adoption that will cause them to stay away, even temporarily. Make sure you have a supportive environment before you enter the process. Otherwise the loss of these friendships may become overwhelming.

• Having children is an outing experience. Be prepared for everyone to know your family structure. It will come up in every interaction you have with new people and those who are just learning of the new addition to your family. If you are not open with others when your child(ren) are present, your children will inherently sense that something is amiss. You certainly don't want to feed any notions of homophobia in your children. They will get plenty negative messages elsewhere!

• Be prepared for silly questions. While children don't generally have issues with labels and names adults certainly do. Many times you will be asked, "so what does your child call you?" "How does your child tell you apart?" (if you are co-parenting). If your child happens to call you by your first name (which many do, at least during different developmental phases) expect others to react. Some think this is something you will have imposed on the child because it is the only way to tell you apart. Some will actually believe (and may even say!) that this is because you are really only pretending to be a family! Most children really don't have an issue, but their parents may still word their questions with, "my child was wondering what your child called you..." We have probably heard it all! In general, your child will come to their own conclusions and personal, comfortable way of addressing you. For some gay couples, both parents are Mom or both are Dad, and the parents know the difference by the intonation or tone of voice. With older children, some will refer to Mom Mary and Mom Grace. Others will use Dad and Daddy.

• Make certain that you and your children are adequately covered in the event of your death or the death of your partner. While the laws in British Columbia now permit for joint adoption of individuals who are not married laws are subject to change and only a legally drawn will can protect you. Please don't rely on your local "free will kit" or even a notary to ensure you are protected. Make the investment of time with a lawyer who specializes in wills and estates and preferably has had their wills tested in the courts.

This article was written specifically for this book. © 2002 Society of Special Needs Adoptive Parents

older parent adoption

> YOU RAISE YOUR KIDS; YOU
> THINK IT'S OVER. NO ONE TELLS
> US IT'S JUST THE BEGINNING.
> – Colorado grandmother

—— Parenting the Second Time Around: ——
How to Deal with Grandparent Adoption
by Jennifer Lee

Grandparent adoption has, for centuries, been a part of human society. From the grandparent who cares for his granddaughter during the work week to the grandparent who legally adopts her grandson, grandparents around the world have had to deal with a myriad of issues in order to meet the needs of their grandchildren, sometimes because the parents have been unable to. While the grandparent-grandchild relationship is a special one and one that most people look forward to, acting as a caregiver can significantly change that relationship and alter what many grandparents thought their retirement years would look like.

Grief and Loss

In some families, parents are unable to care for their children. The reasons for this are hardly ever positive and often, parents are having difficulties with drugs and alcohol or are living in abusive situations. The grandchild is then dealing with the loss of a parent and will experience grief and possibly anger. The child may push her grandparent away and blame him for the loss of her mother or father. As well, grandparents are dealing with their own grief. Many have lost a child to drugs, alcohol or death and in the midst of this grief, suddenly find themselves caring for a young child all over again. They may be too busy dealing with practical issues to fully address their loss.

When dealing with this kind of difficult situation, it is important to look after your own needs, even as you care for your grandchild. Your grandchild's loss is great, but so is yours. Many grandparents have also lost a lifestyle (as we all know, children can change anyone's life) and may have to deal with seeing their friends less or not taking that dream trip to Thailand. Take time out and deal with your grief. It is also worthwhile to seek the help of a support group or organization so that you can speak to others who may have had the same experience.

Aging and Health

As we age, we deal with more and more health issues. Energy is not what it once was and some grandparents may have existing conditions that can flare up unpredictably. While parenting itself is not new for grandparents, the way they physically feel is. A grandmother in her 60s will have a more difficult time keeping up with an active three year old than a woman in her 30s. And thinking about the possibility of contracting a serious illness while your grandchild is still young can cause a lot of stress.

Get lots of help. If you have other children, ask them to take your grandchild for a weekend while you rest and regain your energy. Take advantage of respite care providers and, if it's financially possible, enroll your grandchild into a daycare program for a certain number of hours a week. Take care of yourself and do not neglect your health. Make plans for your grandchild if you fall ill. Make sure that there is someone you trust who can care for the child in the case of emergency. While planning for a catastrophic event is never pleasant, having a firm plan will go a long way in reducing some of your anxiety.

Finances

Many grandparents are living on pensions and government assistance, which, for only one or two people, can be sufficient. When faced with caring for a child who will need clothes, food, dental work and any number of other things, many grandparents may find themselves unable to make ends meet. You may be living in a one-bedroom apartment with three children and unable to afford anything more than basic food, clothing and transportation costs.

Many grandparents have come out of retirement to deal with the extra costs. Others look into alternative funding through the government. Unfortunately, there are no easy answers for the extra financial strain that caring for grandchildren can cause, but remember to look into every avenue that's open to you, whether that's extra government assistance or a part-time job.

Guilt

Many grandparents care for their grandchildren when their children are unable to parent because of drugs, alcohol or violence. Knowing that your child is troubled can often lead to feelings of guilt. What did I do wrong? What could I have done differently? Am I a bad parent?

Remember that the choices you made as a parent were made with the information you had; you did the best you could. Yes, there are always things you could have done differently and the older you get, the more obvious your mistakes from the past become. However, guilt over events that are long past your control is futile. You can only worry about the present. The very persistent needs of your grandchild deserve your full attention.

A Different Connection

While the relationship between grandparents and grandchildren change when adoption becomes an issue, the opportunity exists for that relationship to become even deeper and more complex. The grandparent can connect the child to his or her past and provide a link to the family that is less accessible if the child is taken into foster care. Daily, shared experiences make up a family and it is often the little things, like meals and chores, that help bring individuals together. It is often much easier for the child to be cared for by someone familiar, someone who knows that the child doesn't like tomatoes and needs to have a night light by his bed. Becoming that constant, loving figure in your grandchild's life is important for the child but also hugely rewarding for you.

Few of us plan for extra responsibility as we get older and fewer still expect to be caregivers for our grandchildren. However, when our children become unable to care for their children, many of us would rather step up than see the children go into government care. The question then becomes: how can I be an active parent when I'm approaching my 60s or 70s? The answer isn't easy, but it's simple; we do the best we can.

This article was written specifically for this book. © 2002 Society of Special Needs Adoptive Parents

You're Never Too Old:
The Joys and Challenges of Adoption for Older Parents
by Sara Graefe

Along with the many myths and misconceptions about adoption is the notion that only young couples can adopt. In actual fact, adoptive parents are as diverse a group as any other, coming from different social, economic and cultural backgrounds. Many single people are parents through adoption, as are older folks. Some are grandparents who have become legal guardians or adoptive parents to their birth grandchildren, when their own adult children are no longer able to parent (i.e., due to death, serious illness, substance abuse problems, living in abusive situations, etc.). Others are simply people who want to create a family at this later stage in life. For example, there are single women and couples who weren't able to take time out during the woman's child-bearing years due to career and other pressures, who now have the time and space to create the family they've always wanted. There are empty-nesters who've already raised a family, through birth or adoption, and want to do it all over again. There are those compelled by a humanitarian desire to open their hearts and their homes to youngsters without a permanent family, as a small but significant way of making a difference.

Prospective adoptive parents are often worried that they will be turned away because they're "too old." People hear all kinds of things through the grapevine, including stories of grandparents who've been overlooked by social workers seeking homes for substance exposed infants. However, if you apply to adopt, you can't be turned down simply because you're "too old." The Canadian Charter of Human Rights and Freedoms protects you against discrimination due to age. The *Adoption Act* and current child protection legislation in British Columbia support placements that are in the best interests of the child, and recognize the importance of maintaining kinship ties. This means that as a grandparent, you should be taken into consideration as a potential caregiver for your grandchildren if they cannot return to their birthparent(s). If for some reason you aren't approached outright, you may still petition to adopt the child, so long as you are willing to submit yourself to the scrutiny of social workers and the courts, to prove that living with you is in the child's best interests.

Ultimately, you're the only one who can truly judge whether or not you're "too old" to parent. Ask yourself whether you're ready and able to take on a child at this stage of your life. Look at your strengths, your health, your financial situation, and your capacity to parent before you decide to adopt. It's important to go into the process with realistic expectations.

That said, grandparents often don't have much choice in the matter. You may feel that you have been thrust into the role of surrogate parent because your adult child has lost control of their life (they may be abusing substances, have landed in jail, have been harming the child, etc.), or because they've passed away, either suddenly or after a long illness. As Sylvie de Toledo, US author and founder of the organization Grandparents As Parents, points out: "There are many complicated reasons why grandchildren need grandparents to care for them. But, in the end, the reasons you take them in are straightforward and simple: love, duty, and the bonds of family…. Often you are the only one standing between your grandchild and foster care. I have seen many grandparents disrupt their lives, their finances, and their health to keep their grandchildren together and away from strangers" (*Grandparents As Parents*, New York: Guilford Press, 1995, p. 15).

I recently spoke with Allison Kampman, who lives in Abbotsford, BC. She and her husband spent many years raising their "first family" of birth children, now adults. At 59, she and her husband are now parenting a second time around, as legal guardians of a young child with special needs. Allison spoke to me about some of the joys and challenges facing older people and grandparents who take on parenting responsibilities.

The Hard Stuff

Becoming a new parent at any age is a huge event, bringing with it all the stresses and challenges of a major life change. Taking on a child as you get older brings with it an additional set of challenges.

Although you're never too old to parent, the truth is you have less energy and mobility than you used to – and now you're taking on a twenty-four-hour-a-day, seven-day-a-week job, caring for a child with special needs that require extra attention.

You have to brace yourself for major lifestyle changes. Even those who've already raised a family have likely adjusted to living without children in recent years. The arrival of children into your home is hugely disruptive to your set routine. Suddenly your days are filled with diapers, bag lunches, and getting the kids to school. Your neatly-ordered house may suddenly look like a cyclone's hit, with toys all over the floor and fingerprints on the walls. Instead of enjoying your hard-earned retirement, you may find you can't even stop to hear yourself think, let alone fill your days with your own leisurely pursuits.

Your social life is impacted as well. Friends your own age are enjoying the company of their peers, while you suddenly find yourself interacting with your child's friends, the paediatrician, the teachers at school, and other parents who are often much younger. While your own peers may also have children in their lives, many of them are enjoying being "simply grandparents," while you are weathering the stresses and responsibilities of being a primary caregiver. As Allison puts it, "You find yourself raising a child among your friends' grandchildren." Another grandmother complains, "We don't belong with our old friends, nor do we belong with the young parents of our grandchildren's friends" (*Grandparents As Parents*, p.26).

Raising a child also has financial implications. Suddenly you're faced with extra expenses, for food, clothes, bedding, medical bills, transportation, and even toys – things to meet the child's basic needs. As an older person, you may be retired and relying on a pension or savings, which can make things extra tight financially with a growing child in the house.

Given that you've taken on a child through adoption or guardianship, you're likely grappling with complex special needs issues. Even if your child doesn't have a diagnosed physical condition or disability, they are arriving in your home with baggage from the birth family or previous placement(s). Whether you are parenting a stranger's child or your very own grandchild, your new arrival is experiencing a disrupted attachment, and is grieving the loss of their birth parents who can no longer care for them, for whatever reason. Many of these kids have witnessed violence or have been abused themselves; others have spent chaotic early years with substance abusing parents, and may well be suffering from medical conditions such as FAS and PDE from alcohol or drug exposure in the womb. Often traumatized by their past experiences, these children are prone to acting out, and exhibit a range of challenging behaviours, the likes of which you may have never seen before.

If you're a grandparent who's taken on your grandchildren, you are likely working through your own grief issues, as well. You are grappling with the loss of your own adult child and their inability to parent – be it due to illness or death, serious addiction problems, or abusive or other troubling behaviours. You may experience feelings of guilt and shame about your adult child's actions, and blame yourself for their problems.

Dealing with an addicted or otherwise troubled adult can be stressful and upsetting in itself. You may have witnessed your grown addict go through treatment only to relapse time and time again. Your adult child may flit in and out of your and your grandchild's lives, unreliably. As Sylvie puts it, "These are the parents who show up long enough to make promises, break promises, and disappear again," earning them the title "deadbeat moms and dads" (*Grandparents As Parents,* p.48). You may face additional stress if your adult child regrets or protests the adoption or guardianship order. You may find yourself embroiled in court proceedings which divide the family. You may even be pushed to make the difficult decision of getting a restraining order against your own adult child. If you're dealing with a troubled adult, it's important to set firm boundaries to protect yourself and your grandchild. While it's not productive to blame yourself for your adult child's troubles, you can take steps to stop enabling their behaviour. Set firm rules and stand by them. Set boundaries and learn to say no. Get support for yourself. And, ultimately, you have to learn to let go.

The Silver Lining

Being an older parent also has its benefits. While you may not have the energy and stamina you once had, you may well have more free time in your life. This free time is a precious gift you have to offer – it can be time for teaching, time for listening, time for reading, time for playing, in effect, quality time to connect with your adopted child.

Some older parents actually find that caring for children gives them a new lease on life. Sylvie cites the example of a 300-pound grandmother with diabetes, arthritis, a bad heart and high blood pressure, who woke up one morning and realized she couldn't properly raise a two-year-old flat on her back. Caring for her three grandchildren literally got her back on her feet. Allison, meanwhile, finds that having a child in her life keeps her feeling young-at-heart.

You also bring to your parenting wisdom and perspective that comes with years of life experience. Allison, for example, remembers feeling much more overwhelmed by behavioural issues when she was parenting her first set of kids. "When you're younger, those problems seem bigger, sometimes insurmountable." Having seen her first set of kids to adulthood, she's learned to deal with each crisis as it arises and then let it go, embracing the attitude that "this too shall pass." As an older parent with a young child, she finds that she is much more tolerant and flexible in her expectations, which makes it easier to deal with challenging behaviours as they occur.

As an older person, you may find it easier to work with professionals and advocate for your child. Once again, your years of experience pay off. You've likely dealt with professionals and systems before, either with your earlier children or simply in your own personal life. As a result, you have a set of advocacy and communication skills under your belt that will make the experience less daunting this time around. You may even find that your age commands respect with authority figures. Allison finds that she gets a better reception from teachers and other professionals than she did years ago. "People tend to listen to you and be more polite," Allison laughs. She's found that teachers defer to her experience, treating her like a "buddy" on the same team, enabling them to work together to best meet her child's needs.

And, as Allison and Sylvie both point out, there is love. Love (and a sense of a deep, familial bond) is the main reason why grandparents choose to take on their grandchildren. It is also why older parents choose to adopt at this later stage in life. These parents are opening their hearts as well as their homes, in order to give a child their best shot in life. Allison says, "We had to ask ourselves, 'what is adoption to us?' Not to create a family forever, given our child's specific special needs and shorter life expectancy, and our own age as parents – but to parent this child that no one else will take on."

Get Support

Don't try to do it alone. Parenting at any age is stressful and challenging. Like any parent, you need – and deserve – support.

Respite is essential. Respite means getting a break from your child and the demands of parenting, making alternate care arrangements so you get some temporary rest and relief for yourself. Respite gives you the time and space you need to recharge your batteries, so you can return to your parenting with fresh energy and perspective. All parents caring for children with special needs benefit from respite. Given that you're an older person with less energy to spare, it's especially important that you give yourself a break. You don't want to compromise your health and well-being unnecessarily – after all, your child needs you. Taking a small break on a regular basis will help you hang in there with your child for the long term.

Respite can come in many forms. It can be about hiring a qualified babysitter come to look after your child for an evening, so you and your spouse can spend some quality time together. If you are co-parenting, it can mean trading off child care responsibilities with your partner so one of you gets an afternoon or evening off while the other stays home, and vice-versa. You might also consider trading time with another family raising a child with similar special needs, or with another older adoptive couple. You can also make more formal arrangements, setting up substitute child care or longer term respite care through a social worker or formal program.

Surround yourself with a team of supportive team of people, other family members and friends who are willing to play an active role in your child's life. These are people you can call on when you're reaching your limit and need a break. They are caring individuals who know and understand how to deal with your child's behaviour; people with whom your child is comfortable. You may want to assign these alternate caregivers specific roles, essentially creating a circle of support in your child's life. For example, Allison suggests designating another older person as a surrogate grandparent, someone with whom your child can go to the park, play ball, watch movies, and do all the "fun" stuff that grandparents and grandchildren do together. As the actual grandparent or older adopted parent, you have essentially become the primary caregiver of the child, the person who has to deal with the less-fun stuff, such as day-to-day routines and discipline. While you and your grandchild should also make room for fun, it's a definite bonus if the child has another grandparent-like figure in their life.

Allison also suggests finding a younger adult to participate in your child's life, someone who can play sports and do "the active stuff" with the child if you no longer have the energy or mobility to do so yourself. Allison has a "younger fellow" in her circle who takes on this role with her child. If you don't know any younger people, you might try hooking up with a community-based organization such as Big Brothers or Big Sisters.

When hiring a babysitter, look for someone who has experience dealing with children with special needs. Ordinary babysitters often burn out because they don't have experience with complex conditions and challenging behaviours. Have the sitter come to visit a few times when you are home, and give them tips on how to deal with your child's specific needs and behaviour.

Depending on the situation, your child may still have on-going contact with their birth parent(s). For legal guardians, your guardianship order may include visitation rights. In the case of adoption, you may have negotiated an openness agreement. On-going contact with the parents can be incredibly positive, if boundaries and expectations are clear, and the parents are "fit" or "safe" to be part of your child's life. Allison has found the more she can involve her child's birth mother, the better for all parties. However, if your adult child or the birth parent is still struggling with addictions or other problems, these visits can be extremely stressful for both you and your young child. In this case, it's best to get outside support so you can air your concerns, and re-negotiate visitation ground rules as needed.

Take a parenting course. Some of you might find this idea insulting or patronizing, particularly if you've already raised a family, and/or if you've had to defend in court your right to parent your grandchild. But, as Allison and Sylvie are both quick to point out, parenting has changed from the child-rearing you might have done twenty-five, thirty years ago – as has the society around you. For one thing, kids have changed. In today's fast-paced, media-driven society, children are being pushed to grow up faster than ever. Through television, Internet, and advertising, children are exposed to sex, violence and the world around them at a much earlier age than previous generations. Further, if your adopted child came from a drug-using or abusive home, or lost a parent due to a serious illness or accident, they've already been forced to contend with adult issues before they're ready. Your child may present challenging behaviours caused by the trauma they've experienced, or by other special needs conditions such as FAS, PDE, or ADHD, to name a few.

Meanwhile, parenting standards and expectations have also changed in recent years, particularly with regards to disciplinary techniques. Physical punishment is generally no longer acceptable, and in some cases is even considered abusive, and could be grounds for removing your child from your home. Also, you may have forgotten over the years how children behave, and be out of touch with what is acceptable behaviour and what should be modified. It is helpful, then, to take a class both to refresh yourself and bring yourself up to speed – and to expose yourself to new parenting techniques that help children learn responsibility, accountability, confidence, and self-esteem.

A regular parenting course is a good place to start. Such courses are offered through local community centres and neighbourhood houses, family service agencies, hospitals, and even community colleges. In addition, the Ministry of Children and Family Development's orientation course for prospective adoptive parents is incredibly useful, as it touches on specific issues relating to adoption and special needs. Allison also recommends looking into an infant/toddler child development course at your local community college, to help you better understand and work with your child's special needs. There are also many good parenting books, videos and magazines available to help you out.

Don't isolate. Connect with others. Seek counselling to get support for yourself. Join a support group for adoptive parents, such as those offered through SNAP, so you can hook up with other parents, compare notes, problem-solve, and share stories – your battles as well as your triumphs. There are also support groups specifically geared for grandparents and older parents, run by US-based organizations such as Grandparents As Parents (GAP) and Grandparents United for Children's Rights (see contact information at the end of this article).

Be gentle with yourself and hang in there. As Sylvie reminds us, "It doesn't matter if you are on a picket line or in a grocery line, every grandparent trying to raise a grandchild perseveres. Each morning your grandchildren wake up safe and each night they go to bed well loved and well cared for, you have succeeded." (*Grandparents As Parents*, p.274).

This article was written specifically for this collection. © 2003 Society of Special Needs Adoptive Parents.

For more information about starting a Grandparents' Support Group, or for existing support groups in your area, contact:

Grandparents As Parents (GAP), Sylvie de Toledo, Psychiatric Clinic for Youth, 2801 Atlantic Avenue, Long Beach, CA USA 90801, ph. (213) 595-3151.

Grandparents United for Children's Rights, 137 Larkin Street, Madison, WI 53705 USA, ph. (608) 238-8751 or (608) 236-0480, fax (608) 238-8751.

some parting words

Hang In There

You've already demonstrated your commitment to your child and to yourself by making it this far—by weathering the struggles of parenting a child with special needs, hanging in there no matter how much your child has tested or challenged you, and even just by picking up this book. It's probably been hard, but you've made it this far. Keep on hanging in there the best you can, and don't forget to take care of yourself.

Even if you're faced with what seems like the worst case scenario—the interventions have failed or come too late, the child has left home or the child has been removed from the home—this doesn't mean you've failed as a parent. It is helpful to remember that you're not there to make a person's life—you're there to be with them while they live it. You can help them, hold their hand and support them, but there are some things you cannot control. As Brenda Knight points out (page 155, *A Toolkit for Parents*), being a parent doesn't mean you have to live with the child twenty-four hours a day. Being a parent means being an advocate, somebody sending that child love from somewhere in the world, making sure that the child gets services, and providing a safe place for the child to phone home to. In some circumstances, parenting from a distance is the best way of taking care of yourself and taking care of your child.

resources

Print, Audio & Video Resources

Complete Adoption: Everything You Need to Know to Adopt a Child (2000) Laura Beauvais Godwin and Raymond Godwin.

The Encyclopedia of Adoption (1991) Christine Adamec and William L. Pierce

GRIEF & LOSS

Helping Children Cope with Separation and Loss Revised Edition (1994) Claudia L. Jewett

Twenty Things Adopted Kids Wish Their Adoptive Parents Knew (1999) Sherrie Eldridge

On Children and Death (1983) Elisabeth Kubler-Ross

ATTACHMENT

Attachment: the Root of Our Well Being (2000) Debra Combs (audio)

Can this Child Be Saved (1999) Foster W. Cline and Cathy Helding

Attachment, Trauma, and Healing Understanding and Treating Attachment Disorder in Children and Families (1998) Terry Levy and Michael Orlans

ADOPTION & IDENTITY

Communicating with the Adopted Child (1991) Miriam Komar

Talking With Young Children about Adoption (1993) Mary Watkins and Susan Fisher.

OPEN ADOPTION

Open Adoption Experience (1993) Lois Ruskai Melina and Sharon Kaplan Roszia

Older Child Adoption (1998) Grace Robinson

SEARCH & REUNION

Adoption Reunion Survival Guide, Preparing Yourself for the Search, Reunion and Beyond (2001) Julie Jarrell Bailey and Lynn N. Giddens.

Self Directed Search and Reunion Information (2000) Nina Miller, Diane Roski, Nila Somaia and Loretta Stroh

Birth Bonds: Reunions Between Birth Parents and Adoptees (1989) Judith Gediman and Linda Brown

DISRUPTION

Adoption and Disruption: Rates, Risks and Responses (1988) Richard P. Barth and Marianne Berry

Adoption Disruption (1988) Adoptive Parents Association of Alberta

REDEFINING FAMILY

Dim Sum, Bagels and Grits, a Sourcebook for Multicultural Famililes (2001) Myra Alperson

A Canadian Guide to International Adoptions: How to Find, Adopt,and Bring Home Your Child (1992) John Bowen

Raising Healthy Multiracial Adoptive Families (1999) Harriet Fancott

Grandparenting with Love and Logic; Practical Solutions to Todays Grandparenting Challenges (1994) Foster Cline and Jim Fay

Grandparents as Parents: A Survival Guide for Raising a Second Family (1995) Sylive de Toldeo and Deborah Edler Brown

Lesbian and Gay Parenting Handbook (1993) April Martin

Adoption and Ethics, the Role of Race, Culture, and National Origin (2000) Madelyn Freundlich

Adopting on Your Own, the Complete Guide to Adopting as a Single Parent (2000) Lee Varon

Web Resources

BC Ministry for Children and Family Development: www.mcf.gov.bc.ca/adoption
Adoption Council of Canada: www.adoption.ca
Canada Adopts: www.canadaadopts.com
Canadopt: http://www.canadopt.ca/

North American Council on Adoptable Children: http://www.nacac.org

BC Parent Advisory Committee www.bccpac.bc.ca
Parenting Special Needs: www.familyfocus.com

Association for Treatment and Training in the Attachment of Children: www.attach.org

Organizations

The Society of Special Needs Adoptive Parents (SNAP)
1-800-663-7627, www.snap.bc.ca

Adoption Council of Canada
613-235-0344, www.adoption.ca

North American Council on Adoptable Children
651-644-3036, www.nacac.org

acknowledgements

A book series of this scope would not have been possible without the help of various individuals and organizations. The editor would like to acknowledge the following:

Brad Watson and the Society of Special Needs Adoptive Parents (SNAP), for kick-starting this project, and Susan Lees and the Adoption Support Program at the Queen Alexandra Centre for Children's Health, for support and financial assistance;

The British Columbia Ministry for Children and Family Development, for funding support for the production of this series;

Jennifer Lee of Ben Simon Press, for her editorial, design, and project management; Lissa Cowan, also of Ben Simon Press, for project direction;

Elyssa Schmid of Radiant Design, for her cover designs and layout direction;

Verna Booth in the SNAP library, for research assistance and long hours spent compiling the resource lists;

Emilie Cameron and Neil Carey, for additional research support;

Dolores Talavera, Maria Mercado-Koyanagi, Neil Carey and SNAP office volunteers, for their help securing reprint permission for various articles;

Susan Cowan, Coordinator of Volunteer Programs at SNAP, for liaising with contributing adoptive parents;

The many adoptive families and professionals who were willing to contribute their expertise and personal stories for this collection;

And the many authors and publishers who allowed us to use their material in this series. Specific copyright acknowledgement follows each individual article.

contributors

Geoffrey Ainsworth, M.D. Ch.B. FRCPC, is a child psychiatrist, working at BC Children's Hospital, providing inpatient and outpatient consultation services as well as running a private practice. He provides outreach psychiatry services to Northern British Columbia and Yukon. He is the psychiatric director of the Children's Day Treatment Programme, a specialised school setting for children between kindergarten and grade 3, many of whom suffer from reactive attachment disorder.

Ann M. Angel is an adoptive parent of four children and author of *Real For Sure Sister* (Perspectives Press, Inc.). She lives in Wisconsin.

Michael Colberg, together with his partner Gene Parseghian, are the parents through adoption of their teenage daughter Rachel. Colberg is an attorney and clinical social worker and works as a therapist, teacher and clinical mediator in New York City. His practice focuses on the needs of people whose lives have been touched by adoption.

Lissa Cowan is the Editorial Director of Ben Simon Press, Managing Editor of *Family Groundwork Magazine*, and Communications Consultant for SNAP Promotions. She lives on Vancouver Island and works part-time as a writer and translator. She is currently working on a French to English poetry translation.

Helen Creamore has served the adoption community for many years as a Resource Parent and Director of SNAP.

Bob Creasy, M.S.W., R.S.W. worked for many years as a senior counsellor at the Adoption Reunion Registry, Family Services of Greater Vancouver. He is currently based in Alberta.

Ro de Bree is a long-time SNAP resource parent living in Duncan, BC. She has written and published extensively about her experiences parenting adoptive children with Fetal Alcohol Syndrome.

Leah Dobell lives and works in Vancouver, BC. Her life has been touched by adoption in many ways: her youngest brother was adopted into her Caucasian family from Korea at the age of two. Leah is now the proud adoptive single mom of Floyd, a $2^1/_2$-year-old Aboriginal boy who has partial FAS. She is also a foster parent and works outside the home as a Registered Nurse.

Harriet Fancott is a writer, editor and webmaster who served the adoption community for many years as the Communications Coordinator for the Adoptive Families Association of BC where she edited *Focus on Adoption Magazine* and created the book, *Raising Healthy Multiracial Adoptive Famililes*. She now works as a web designer.

Gladys Fraser, PFP, STI. AICB, is a long time SNAP board member and resource parent residing in the sunny Okanagan. She and her partner have experienced the process of adopting and raising a special needs child in BC. Her professional work as a bank manager and financial planner with Scotiabank have contributed to her understanding of the financial issues surrounding adoption and post-adoptive support. Gladys regularly volunteers to assist families and individuals with financial survival and planning issues.

Ellen S. Glazer is a social worker and adoption counselor. She lives in Newton, Massachusetts with her family.

Sara Graefe served the adoption community for five years in her role as SNAP's former Publications Coordinator. She is the editor and principal writer of SNAP's best-selling book, *Parenting Children Affected by Fetal Alcohol Syndrome: A Guide for Daily Living.* She currently works in Vancouver as a freelance writer, and in the story department of *Edgemont,* CBC's television series for youth.

Ellen Halliday is a legal assistant who volunteered for many years as a contributing writer with SNAP.

Tanya Helton-Roberts, M.Sc., has over ten years experience in working with families with special needs children. She has worked with parents, police, schools, organizations, social services, and mental health agencies to develop attachment-based responses to special needs children. Through her office Forest Cottage Coaching in Fort St. John, BC, Tanya provides life coaching to clients, in-person and over the phone. The sibling of three adoptive children and the parent of an adopted child (her niece), Tanya brings practical understanding as well as a caring heart to her work.

Sharon Jinkerson is a filmmaker and reunited adult adopted person. She lives on Pender Island, BC. Her film *Inside the Mask: a Journey from Darkness into Light* is about the adoptio of Aboriginal children into non-Aboriginal homes.

Patricia Irwin Johnston, M.S., is the publisher of Perspectives Press, a publishing house that offers books related to reproductive health education, and adoption information and education. The adoptive parent of three, she has been writing, speaking, and advocating about infertility and adoption issues for 20 years.

Katherin Jones, B.Ed., is the mother of two sons through intercountry adoption. She founded *Adoption Helper* magazine in 1990 with publisher Robin Hilborn, and became the publication's first editor. She currently works as a public school teacher in Toronto, and has appeared in public forums, seminars and the media as an adoption advocate.

Deborah C. Joy, author of *Benjamin Bear Gets a New Family*, is in private practice in Cincinnati, Ohio, as an adoption therapist. She is the single parent of four children.

Sharon Kaplan Roszia directs a successful and innovative program for the Kinship Center of California whose mission it is to recruit, educate, match, place and support families who are willing to foster/adopt the children who have waited the longest in the foster care system. Roszia entered the field of foster care and adoption in 1963 and has worked in both the public and private sectors as well as in private practice. She has lectured extensively both domestically and abroad, written two books and several articles, and produced many training videos and audio tapes. She is a parent by birth, fostering, and adoption.

Jennifer Lee is the General Manager of Ben Simon Press, Editor in Chief of *Family Groundwork Magazine* and Communications Consultant for SNAP Promotions. She is currently working on her second novel and an online arts magazine for youth.

Bruce Leslie was the principal drafter of the Strategic Plan for Aboriginal Services under the former Ministry for Children and Families (2000) and served as the Implementation Manager and Senior Policy Advisor with the Aboriginal Relations Branch, Ministry for Children and Families. Bruce has a background in psychology, and received his MA in Indigenous Governance from the University of Victoria.

Susan MacRae is originally from Edmonton, Alberta. She has a BFA in Creative Writing from the University of British Columbia and is presently working on her Master's degree in English/Creative Writing at City College in Harlem, USA. She has been a volunteer writer for SNAP since 1997.

Rebecca Perbix Mallos is in private practice at the Attachment Center Northwest, and on staff at the Adoption Resource Center, Children's Home Society of Washington. She is a popular speaker throughout the US and Canada for her work on the interface between trauma and attachment in special needs adoption. She is a parent by birth, adoption and fostering.

Lois Melina is one of the country's leading experts on raising adopted children. Her books are required reading at many adoption agencies. She is also a frequent speaker at conferences and workshops across North America, and writes a regular column, "Adopted Child," for *Adoptive Families* magazine.

Elizabeth Newman is a Registered Clinical Counsellor at Choices Adoption and Counselling Services in Victoria, BC. Her article "Openness: Benefits and Risks" is based, in part, on her master's thesis on open adoption.

Robert O'Connor

Bruce Regier is a social worker with Hope Pregnancy and Adoption Services in Abbotsford, BC.

Stuart Rennie is a social worker with the BC Ministry of Children and Family Development. He serves adoptive families in Vancouver and the Lower Mainland.

Mary Runte is a lecturer at the University of Lethbridge. Mary has worked for several years in social services, providing support to families with special needs children.

Marlou Russell, Ph.D. is a psychologist specializing in adoption issues in Santa Monica, California. Dr. Russell is an adopted person in reunion with her birth family and the author of *Adoption Wisdom: A Guide to the Issues and Feelings of Adoption.*

Deborah N. Silverstein, LCSW is Associate Director of Kinship Center. She has been with Kinship Center since 1993 and has worked in each of the program centers. She is a co-founder of the Southern California programs. Deborah is herself an adoptive parent of special needs youngsters, as well as a grandparent. She received her Masters in Social Work in 1981 from the University of Southern California, specializing in work with children and families. She has worked as a psychotherapist since that time.

Along with being adopted herself, **Chris Simpson** has a husband who was adopted as part of a sibling group of three. They have four birth children and three years ago, adopted a sibling group of two. They recently adopted a sibling group of three with extreme abuse issues.

also available from snap & ben simon press

Adoption Piece by Piece (3 volumes):
> **Lifelong Issues**
> **Special Needs**
> **A Toolkit for Parents**

Edited by Sara Graefe

This series represents a comprehensive collection of articles from experienced parents and professionals on a variety of topics related to adoption.

Living with Prenatal Drug Exposure: A Guide for Parents
By Lissa Cowan and Jennifer Lee

This comprehensive book for parents and professionals introduces caregivers to the challenges of caring for a child prenatally exposed to drugs.

Living with FASD: A Guide for Parents, 3rd Edition
By Sara Graefe

This updated 3rd edition includes diagnostic criteria, special considerations for infants and adolescents, and an expanded resource list.

Adoptive Families are Families for Keeps
Text by Lissa Cowan, illustrations by Stephanie Hill

This colouring book will provide social workers, foster parents, caregivers and educators with dynamic and instructive ways to introduce and discuss a wide range of adoption issues with young children.

To order any of these titles, please visit our website at www.snap.bc.ca.